P9-BJU-680

EDWARD THE RAKE

EDWARD THE RAKE

An Unwholesome
Biography of
Edward VII

by
John Pearson

Harcourt Brace Jovanovich
New York and London

Printed in the United States of America

Library of Congress Cataloging in Publication Data
Pearson, John, 1930–
    Edward the rake.
    Bibliography: p.
    1. Edward VII, King of Great Britain, 1841–1910.
I. Title.
✓ DA567.P4   941.082′092′4 [B]   75–1450
    ISBN 0–15–127965–9

First American edition

B C D E

FOR JULIA, WITH LOVE.

Contents

EDWARD THE RAKE

"That Dreadful Business at the Curragh"

1

As a womanizer, Albert Edward, Prince of Wales, had the most terrible beginner's luck. Had the Almighty—with God-like eye upon the future—set out to read the Royal Heir a lesson on the dangers of the flesh, He could hardly have acted in a more thunderous, high Victorian style. The loss of the royal virginity was accompanied by such calamities, such wailing and reproach from those he loved, that it was as if the Lord were privately lamenting all of the trouble that the Prince would bring the Godly. It was a dramatic start for a lifetime's lechery.

It was doubly impressive for being unexpected. Certainly the Prince had no idea what he was in for on the June morning in 1861 when he embarked for Ireland and all the regimental splendors of the Curragh Camp. He was just nineteen and had always longed to be a soldier. Now he was off at last on military maneuvers. It had been planned with all the care that went with the arrangements for the Royal

Family, and the Prince's visit was important for the Curragh, the mini-Aldershot some twenty miles from Dublin and seat of the British military presence in the island. The camp was full. The Grenadiers were stationed there that year, and on the twenty-sixth of August, at the culmination of God-knows-what excesses of unsullied military zeal, Victoria herself would come to take the salute at a full-scale sovereign's parade. For the Queen this would be a family affair. Her adored Consort at her side, she would be seeing their eldest son in his first public military role. He had been recently commissioned lieutenant-colonel in the Grenadiers and would be marching with his men. For Victoria this would naturally be a source of pride—and also of relief. "Bertie," as he was called at home, had always been a problem, but he was clearly trying to be good. His dear father's plans for him were working out.

It was Albert who had realized his son's military ambitions and who had promised the commission in the Guards as a prize for good behavior and success at lessons. And Bertie had evidently tried. He was no scholar; at times his family considered him half-witted. But he had recently stuck man-fully to his father's careful plans for finishing his education— six months at Oxford, where he was chaperoned and guarded night and day, followed by an equalizing six months at Cambridge. Quite what his saintly father hoped for from this brisk exposure to the doubtful learning and more doubtful morals of mid-Victorian Oxbridge is not clear; but Albert had a touching faith in some sort of educational osmosis, very much in line with his scientific optimism, by which his son would naturally absorb the essential qualities of learning and high-mindedness to which he was exposed.

By summer 1861 the Prince's university career was nearly over. He must have been relieved. For in these seats of learning he had been both pampered and restrained—guarded by tutors, lectured by regius professors, sermonized by bishops, exhorted by long letters from his father, and constantly watched over by his male nanny, the indefatigable General Robert Bruce, whose main task was to keep Bertie out of trouble. It must have all been curiously unreal, for he was more or less cut off from other undergraduates and like some Japanese emperor or god-king living in their midst. At both places he had lived in his own private residence; Albert the Good was realist enough to know what would have happened to his boy had he been given rooms in college.

At this time he was still very much an unknown quantity. People who met him generally liked him. He had a natural charm and was invariably polite. He was short, like his mother, having stopped growing at five feet, six inches, and already rather plump. (At Cambridge the Prince Consort warned him against overeating, saying that it would spoil his figure, which it did.) But the general impression was of his innocence and of his eagerness for life. The Winterhalter portrait of a year before shows an unformed, rather wistful face. The pale blue eyes stare sadly; the receding chin is not yet protected by its beard. He still had something of a stammer, and it must have been hard not to feel a little sorry for him—even when he won his great reward, and the royal tailor came and measured him for his splendid scarlet uniform and he was brought his bearskin and his greatcoat and his gleaming boots—plus the gazetting as staff-colonel with the Grenadiers. His future as planned by Albert was already falling into place, and since he was "both Prince of the Blood and Heir to the Throne," he had to have a rank to match his future role in life.

But it was not that simple—with Bertie nothing ever was—and even his appointment to the Grenadiers had to fall between the two extremes of easy eminence and nannylike control that had been dogging him since adolescence. He could not possibly take his appointment like an ordinary young officer, mix with his comrades (which he would have loved), and calmly follow through his military career. Nor, on the other hand, could he be left to make the most of all the rank and privilege to which his status entitled him. This would not have chimed in with his father's strenuous belief in self-improvement. Bertie must make a show of *earning* his exalted rank. He had to prove himself and work. Above all, he must suffer. It was to make sure that he did that the Prince Consort engineered one of his famous *plans*.

It was all carefully worked out. A memorandum was composed; Albert was the sort of man who believed in memoranda, even when dealing with his children. Both Bertie and the commander in chief had to initial it. At the Curragh, the Prince-colonel would occupy the quarters of a brigadier, would have six servants, and, to learn something of the social side of life, would give dinner parties in his quarters to selected senior officers at least twice a week.

But at the same time the Prince had to "earn" his rank by meticulously learning, as Albert's memorandum stated, "all the duties of every grade from ensign upwards." It was pure self-improvement, à la Samuel Smiles,* with a fortnight to suffice for Bertie to master every grade; by the time the Queen arrived, he would have learned enough to command a whole battalion and to maneuver a brigade in the field.

The schedule seems forbidding, but the Prince was delighted with the plan and reached Ireland eager to start his

---

* Samuel Smiles (1812-1904) was the foremost Victorian advocate of the gospel of work and self-improvement through unfettered individual enterprise. His most famous book, *Self-Help*, published in 1859, was one of the great Victorian best sellers.

longed-for military career. In Dublin the Viceroy greeted him and crowds turned out to cheer him; at the Curragh life began in earnest. It was far tougher than he, or his father, had thought, and by mid-August Colonel Percy, his commanding officer, was telling the heir to the throne, "You are too imperfect in your drill, Sir. Your word of command is indistinct. I will *not* try to make the Duke of Cambridge think you more advanced than you are."

One admires the Colonel's frankness, but feels sorry for the Prince. For on the twenty-sixth, when his fond parents came to hold the review of all their troops, Bertie had no brigade—nor even the battalion he had hoped for—and as he marched past his mother he was in the merest subaltern's position, where the shortcomings of his voice would hardly matter. It was a genuine humiliation, although Victoria did write that evening to her uncle Leopold in Belgium saying that "Bertie hadn't looked so very small" in his uniform and that he had acquitted himself "as well as could be expected in the circumstances." This was slight consolation, but Bertie's brother officers had an idea of their own to divert him from his disappointment.

The sexual initiation of princes clearly has its problems—which in franker ages were dealt with carefully. Louis XIV had his first mistress provided for him at the age of fifteen simply to keep him out of trouble. Charles II lost his virginity at sixteen to a discreet but willing Lady while on the isle of Jersey. In both cases, the arrangement kept the young men satisfied until they were needed for full state marriages. Bertie had no such luck. All that the Court could offer him was abstinence—until he married. Certainly the whole idea of princely fornication in the meantime would have been quite unthinkable. Albert had ordered Bertie's tutor, Gibbs, to sketch out the facts of life—with what sort of detail is uncertain—when he was seventeen. And that, as far as Albert was concerned, was that.

Bertie thought otherwise, and was hardly likely to have been satisfied with a sex talk and the promise of an early marriage. As he proved quite conclusively in later life, he was abundantly endowed with all the fleshly appetites of the Hanoverians. He was fascinated by the other sex—and plainly he was hideously frustrated. The prudishness of Windsor, coupled with all the fuss and prying done by General Bruce to preserve his "purity," must have made temptation doubly alluring.

When he arrived among the bold guardees of Curragh Camp, it was as if Victorian morality were sending its hostage into the land of Sodom and Gomorrah. For it would have been hard to find a group more totally opposed to everything Victoria and Albert thought of as morality than among the rich and self-indulgent gentlemen of the Brigade of Guards. Theirs was still the world, for all intents and purposes, of the old Duke of Wellington, of randy memory, a world in which a mistress or two, like a horse, was part of the young officer's everyday equipment.

One of these ladies in attendance on the First Regiment of Grenadiers that summer was the young actress Nellie Clifden. Some of the young officers smuggled her past General Bruce's nose and into the Prince's quarters. He found her waiting for him like a birthday present when he went to bed —and by all accounts he made the most of her. It was a hazardous—and nearly a disastrous—way for the future King of England to learn the real facts of life; for this friendly action by his brother officers caused the unhappy Bertie such a load of obloquy and guilt during the weeks ahead that he must have wished that they had shown their sympathy in some less blatant manner.

Not much is known about the lovely Nellie Clifden, the "soiled rose" who had the honor of inaugurating the long and strenuous career of this most famous royal rake. She was brunette and in her early twenties. Not quite a tart, nor quite a real actress, either, she followed the young officers around and was well known in such fashionable London sin spots as Cremorne Gardens and Mott's Dancing Rooms. One quality that she possessed, apart from looks, availability, and health (no one was going to risk giving the Prince of Wales a dose of clap; that would have been too much even for the cheerful fellows of the Brigade of Guards), was indiscretion. Like many of her successors, Miss Clifden was all too well aware of the honor the royal penis had conferred on her. And so, inevitably, she talked.

She boasted of her conquest around town. The scandal and the interest grew. Not since the days of Queen Victoria's wicked uncles had the ladies of the town enjoyed royal patronage; by mid-September the news had spread through the London clubs, and it was then a mere matter of time before it found its way to Windsor. In the event, Lord Torrington, an established gossip and official gentleman in waiting, felt it his patriotic duty to inform Prince Albert that his son had been sleeping with an actress. All hell, predictably, broke loose.

To start with, the Prince Consort played it fairly cool, taking a "more in sorrow than in anger" line and having the sense to keep the news from Queen Victoria. But to Bertie he made no bones about the anguish his son had caused him. It was, he wrote, "the greatest pain I have yet felt in this life." But even so, Albert's penchant for a memorandum was not deserting him. With Teutonic thoroughness, he had a searching inquiry carried out into what had happened, an inquiry that proved conclusively that Torrington was right and Bertie had hideously fallen. The pain, the "Terrible pain," was too great to permit Albert to meet his erring son for the present, but General Bruce had nobly agreed to overlook the Prince's deception and act as go-between. Bertie must tell the General everything for everybody's sake. Apparently he did—except for the actual names of the officers who had smuggled Nellie into bed with him—and within a few days Albert was writing with paternal forgiveness, urging Bertie to "fight a valiant fight" in future and telling him that his father now felt able to discuss the frightful subject face to face.

Albert's attitude by now was that the incident proved that his son's one hope of real salvation lay in instant marriage. Like Saint Paul, he emphatically believed that it was "better to marry than to burn." "You must not, you dare not be lost," he wrote. "The consequences for this country and for the world would be too dreadful!" To plead such lofty sentiments in person, Albert took a special train to Cambridge the following day.

The Prince, who was in the last few weeks of his condensed university career, was much impressed. They talked. They walked together. Full forgiveness followed, and next day Albert steamed back to London, happy that he and a repentant Bertie now saw eye to eye.

For both of them, the worst was still to come.

Albert had not been well for several weeks. On his return from Cambridge he complained of headaches and catarrh and body pains. He could not sleep. On December 2 he collapsed, and twelve days later he died. The cause of death was typhoid, badly diagnosed and dubiously treated. There was no doubt of this at all. But for the frantic Queen the death was not that simple. For she had nursed her angel during those hideous days, and listened to his sad cries in delirium. From them she had learned the truth about Miss Clifden. That fatal trip to Cambridge had exhausted Albert, and his sleepless nights were racked with worry for his son. He may have died of typhoid, but, as she sorrowfully told her friend Colonel Francis Seymour a few weeks later, what had really killed poor Albert had been "that dreadful business at the Curragh."

From the Queen's letters and remarks, it is quite clear that at this period she saw her son as something of a parricide. The sins of the son had fallen on the blameless father. "Oh, that boy," she wrote, "much as I pity, I never can or shall look at him without a shudder." Kindly Seymour did his best, in a man-of-the-world way, to convince the Queen that Bertie had simply fallen for "a youthful error that very few young men escape." Victoria still shuddered. This was no "youthful error." This was a "fall" so hideous that it confirmed her worst fears and premonitions for her son.

For small, plump Bertie, this must all have been deeply distressing. Much as he had suffered from his father, he had undoubtedly been quite fond of him, and it was ludicrous to cast him as the villain in such a melodrama. But his behavior now is most instructive for the future. He did his best to comfort the distraught Victoria—this despite her "shudders" at his presence. He played the dutiful, affectionate son as well as anyone could wish. "I will be all I can to you" were his first words to her after his father's death. But he refused to overdo it, nor would he indulge in orgies of repentance. This was what upset the Queen, and she wrote to her eldest daughter complaining about "how little depth of feeling about anything" there was in Bertie.

And, in a sense, Victoria was right. He was not a person

of deep feeling, nor was he troubled by remorse or guilt. He was essentially a realist, who knew exactly what he wanted. He took account of people's feelings, but he was not deflected by them. A weaker young man might have been permanently scarred by what had happened, but Bertie evidently had more resilience than anyone expected.

The Making of a Royal Rake

Bertie's education is one of the great cautionary tales of Victorian morality, and in a sense his distraught mama was right when she saw his "fall" with Nellie Clifden as considerably more than just a youthful error. It was a betrayal—of almost everything that she and Albert had believed in. Albert had tried so hard with him, given his moral education so much earnest thought, been so concerned to *make* him good, that something had clearly gone dreadfully wrong. But what?

For us it is easier to find an answer than for Queen Victoria, who could not bear to face the truth. Bertie had obviously kicked, and, in his somewhat stolid German way, he continued to kick for the remainder of his life. With anybody else it would have seemed quite commonplace—and quite predictable, particularly in a family like his, with its long tradition of enmity between the parents and their children. But the significance of Bertie's kicks was, from the start, far wider than it would have been with anybody else. He had been nursed and nurtured in the hothouse of the Royal Family, so that his kicking looked like shattering the windows. This was a danger so appalling that one can understand Victoria's concern.

For the achievement of Victoria and Albert had been in large part a *moral* one. This was their strength. As a married couple, they had virtually rebuilt the English monarchy on the unyielding rock of English earnestness. They had been fortunate. Much of their success came from the way their characters and situation happened to coincide with the emergent conscience of their time—that of the earnest, money-making, and monogamous middle classes. But, just as Bertie was to react against his parents when his moment came, so had their own high moral purpose started originally as a reaction against the elders of their childhood.

As an extremely young princess, living in Kensington Palace, Victoria had witnessed the seamier side of royalty in the late-middle-age excesses of her "wicked uncles," the remaining sons of George III. The Hanoverians, en masse, were an unedifying crew. There was her uncle Clarence, with his ten acknowledged illegitimate children. There was her rakish uncle Cumberland. Her own father, the aggrieved and pompous Duke of Kent, who died when she was six months old, had been persuaded to desert his aging mistress to wed the Princess Leiningen, Victoria's mother, only by the prospect of a parliamentary grant of £25,000 a year. And finally, and wickedest of all, her "Uncle King," old George IV, "swollen, gouty, bewigged, and bedaubed," must have appeared the living embodiment of sin. When she was six, this old apparition, all that was left now of the one-time "first gentleman of Europe," had summoned her to Windsor, where he had quizzed her and then kissed her on the cheek in the

presence of his last mistress, the formidable Lady Conyng-
ham.

Victoria's whole childhood had been saddened by scandal,
and on her accession, of her own accord, she had decided that
what the country needed was "a strict court and a 'high' attitude in herself." She was more than ready for the passionate
uxoriousness of married life with Albert.

He, in his turn, had buttressed her moral sense, and as a
child had actually suffered the effects of "immorality" within
his family. Indeed, the whole example of his family must
have convinced young Albert that sexual license led to personal catastrophe. While he was still a child, his mother left
his father for another man, then died; her name was never
mentioned in his presence. His father, the debauched old
Duke Ernest of Coburg, had led a rackety, cantankerous
existence, while his brother suffered most uncomfortably from
syphilis, which he contracted twice after undisclosed excesses in Berlin. Hardly surprisingly, all these family mis-
fortunes brought out a certain priggishness in Albert; he
believed resolutely in self-control, self-help, and the sacra-
ment of marriage. His wife inevitably felt the same, and soon
they were seeing themselves as chosen instruments of the Almighty, leading the nation in the ways of truth.

All this aroused a certain ridicule in the unregenerate—
particularly among the old aristocracy, many of whom enjoyed the looser attitudes of the turn of the century. Albert
was called a prude, a "thoroughly dreary fellow," a "hu-
mourless German." The Royal Family in turn moved steadily
away from fashionable society and hardened their hearts
against all forms of moral laxity.

This was, in fact, a source of strength. It gave Victoria and
Albert the profoundest sense of purpose. If God was for

them, who could successfully stand against them? Moreover, they were shrewdly aware that respectability paid. The rakish dynasties of Europe seemed to have had their day. Whatever the aristocracy might say was quite beside the point; the emergent classes would not long tolerate corrupt and morally bankrupt regimes. The 1848 revolutions, which shook the rest of Europe, had served to emphasize the dangers. The *métier du roi* was hazardous; royalty's best hope for the future lay in hard work and pure living, precepts that Victoria and Albert, like the true professionals they were, used as the basis for their regenerate English monarchy.

They took the whole task seriously. These were the standards they applied throughout their court—to their followers, to their friends, and also to the education of their children, Bertie in particular. He, after all, was no ordinary child. As the Queen's heir, he was the monarchy's essential hope for the future. In him his parents' work would stand or fall, and in the future much would depend upon how much he embodied all the qualities they lived by—morality, hard work, applied intelligence. In short, the more young Bertie could be made a duplicate of Albert now, the better.

Small wonder, then, that from the beginning Albert and Victoria were such extremely anxious parents, endlessly concerned with Bertie's character. Was he resembling Papa or was the dreaded Hanoverian strain beginning to appear? Could they detect faint echoes of old Cumberland and Clarence and of frightful George IV within the childish temperament? It would have been hard not to worry. As a small boy, Bertie was fractious and temperamental. As he grew older he showed no aptitude for lessons. This was all in disturbing contrast with his older sister, the Crown Princess Victoria. Earnest and good and eager for her lessons, "Vicky" already was a tiny female Albert in the making. She was the only one of Victoria's eight children who was not in awe of her papa. Bertie remained devoted to her, although, ironically, by her marriage to Prince Frederick of Prussia, she was to become the mother of his nephew and future bugbear, the Kaiser William II of Germany. In character Bertie was quite the opposite of Vicky and patently a Hanoverian; the Queen described him sadly as "my caricature."

She could appreciate his virtues, too. All her life this strange ambivalence continued. On his ninth birthday, she admitted to her diary that there was "much good in him. He has such affectionate feeling—great truthfulness and great simplicity of character." But this, alas, was not enough for the great role he had to play. There could be but one solution, the great Victorian panacea—education.

Bertie's education has much to answer for. It was planned with quite implacable high-mindedness, zeal, and a solemn sense of public responsibility. From the very beginning, the ever-methodical Albert naturally consulted all the best authorities, but it was his friend and mentor, the renowned and forbidding Baron Stockmar* whose advice formed the basis for the elaborate educational strait-jacket in which young Bertie was to sweat and suffer for the next twelve years.

According to Stockmar's sage advice the *system* had to ensure that the Prince as future "executive Governor of the

* Baron Christian Frederick Stockmar was something of a gray eminence to the Royal Family. By training a doctor, he established an unrivaled position as personal adviser to Victoria's uncle, Leopold of the Belgians. Then in 1837 he came to England and became unofficial private secretary to the Queen. His influence was behind much of Victoria's authoritarian high-mindedness, and even more so with the Prince Consort. Stockmar was responsible for many of his schemes for social betterment and self-improvement. Always self-confident, he felt that he knew best for Britain and her monarchy.

State," as he described him, would become "the repository of all the moral and intellectual qualities by which it is held together and under the guidance of which it advances in the great path of civilisation." More fulsome still, Bishop Wilberforce replied that "the great object in view is to make him the most perfect man." Only Melbourne, now ancient, ventured a more cautious answer, warning that education rarely achieved "as much as is expected from it." He was not heeded. Too much was now at stake and the royal educators embarked on the great work of creating a "perfect" Prince of Wales.

Their optimism, energy, and the sheer scale of their labors are reminiscent of the efforts of the great mid-Victorian engineers. Everything was possible. Method and effort would conquer all! Science and chemistry, handwriting, geography, scripture and literature and classics and religion—the great system worked out by the tireless Prince Consort was under way. Bertie was obviously no easy subject. His first tutor, Henry Birch, a former captain of the school at Eton, found him "extremely disobedient, impertinent to his masters and unwilling to submit to discipline." Sometimes he showed dumb insolence—a favorite offense—and had to be severely punished. His moods were variable. Despite all this, Birch had apparently liked the Prince, opining that he would ultimately "turn out a *good* and in my humble opinion, a *great* man." Birch taught the Prince until the age of ten, and then departed. The Prince mourned his going, particularly when he met his successor, the humorless, pedantic Frederick Waymouth Gibbs. With Gibbs upon the scene, the system now had teeth.

For seven hourly periods, six days a week, poor Bertie labored, and was now being worked harder than any schoolboy in the land. Worse still, he had no real contact with other boys. The Prince was far too valuable to risk in the rough and tumble of normal children. As Queen Victoria put it, "I have a great fear of young and carefully brought up boys mixing with older boys and indeed with any boys in general." As a slight concession, Albert took him and his brother Alfred to the Eton speech days, but this was not a great success. Nor were his actual lessons. Despite the labors of his teachers, Bertie was not progressing as he should. Sometimes he had tantrums, sometimes he showed signs of extreme fatigue. Everybody worried, and during these crises "Prince Albert would rise early, light his German student's lamp with its green silk shade and tabulate his son's future."

Albert was not the man to weaken—nor was the indefatigable Gibbs. To combat fears that Bertie might be mentally retarded, a phrenologist, the great Dr. Combe, called at Windsor to examine the princely cranium and was sanguine. The Prince's intellectual and moral bumps were steadily enlarging. Parental fears were quite uncalled-for as the brain's "higher powers of control" would certainly expand as well. Albert presumably took heart: the system burgeoned.

Fresh subjects swelled the syllabus—horse-riding, bricklaying at Osborne, gymnastics under the direction of a sergeant. Bertie was made to keep a journal which both Gibbs and Albert examined regularly. And at the end of every day Gibbs compiled a meticulous report of the day's progress—or the lack of it—which was then duly studied by the parents. Hardly surprisingly, as Bertie's biographer records, "Gibbs was really hated by the Prince of Wales."

But Bertie was forced to keep his feelings to himself. The system had him in its iron grip—temporarily at least—and he learned to go along with it. On April Fool's Day, 1858, he was confirmed in St. George's Chapel, Windsor. This was the high point of his parents' hopes for both his moral and religious future; predictably, they made the most of it. The service went off, as even Albert admitted, "with great solemnity" in the presence of the Court, the Prime Minister, Lord John Russell, and Lord Palmerston. Bertie had previously been catechized for more than an hour on his beliefs as a Christian.

"The examination," as the Queen reported to her uncle Leopold, "was long and difficult, but Bertie answered extremely well." And Bishop Wilberforce, who performed the confirmation, now had a chance to see how well the system was progressing in its task of bringing Bertie up to perfect manhood. The Queen described the princely bearing as "gentle, good and proper." Albert added that he hoped the occasion "would make an abiding impression on his mind."

It needed to, for the outside world was waiting and no one, not even Albert, could make it wait much longer as the Prince started to become increasingly aware of its delights. Albert did his best, of course. The parental reins were lengthened—on occasion quite considerably, as when the Prince went off on brief *educational* trips abroad—but always the ends stayed firmly tied to Windsor.

The trouble was not merely that gentle Bertie was so endlessly constrained, but that the constraints were so well meant and yet so resolutely tedious. When he arrived to see his sister Vicky in Berlin, there were already instructions waiting there from Father just to make sure that he kept up his study every day and that his sister read him suitably improving books in the afternoon. When, at seventeen, Bertie went to Rome, Ruskin was consulted on "how best to imbue the Prince with artistic sentiment."* Bertie had fondly hoped to

---

* Ruskin replied, unhelpfully, that he "should be warned against regarding art as a mere means of luxury and pride."

meet King Victor Emmanuel, the dashing *Re Galantuomo,* who had so impressed him once at Windsor with his saber, with which he claimed he could decapitate an ox. No such luck! A visit to the royal court at Turin might put at risk young Bertie's virtue (although Cavour remarked that if he brought *"cette qualité précieuse"* to Turin, he certainly wouldn't lose it there). Instead the disappointed Prince had to seek consolation in lunch with Robert Browning at the British Embassy and earnest walks among the recent excavations on the Appian Way.

Bertie reached eighteen with the system still holding sway. Albert was not the sort that gives up easily, and the great work of earnestly improving Bertie was clearly incomplete. He was given his own establishment—a Georgian mansion in Richmond Park, suitably distant from the delights of London, and another memorandum from Prince Albert, with a set of most rigorous disciplinary rules for Bertie's equerries. They were to teach him "the frivolity and foolish vanity of dandyism," and by their good example stop him adopting "lounging ways such as lolling in armchairs or sofas" or a "slouching gait with hands in the pockets." He must not smoke, of course, or maintain personal relations with anyone except those in official attendance on him. The Prince's future, Albert pointed out, depended on his mixing with "what is commonly called a 'good set.' " Bertie must have laughed at that in years to come, as well as at another of his father's apothegms: "A *practical joke* should never be permitted."

Just to make sure that all these rules were carefully enforced, Bertie was now saddled with a private governor. This is where Colonel (soon to be General) Bruce arrived on the scene. Gibbs departed, but the change in personnel led to no slackening of purpose—rather the reverse. Within a few days Bruce was writing Albert the inevitable letter about Bertie's "wilfulness and constitutional irritability," but added, like so many of his kind before, that "the Prince is really anxious, I think, to improve himself although the process is but slow and uncertain."

The Prince, in fact, was really anxious for one thing and for that alone—to escape the system and enjoy himself as soon as possible. His father must have known this quite well, but he was still desperately hanging on, as parents do, and trusting in the power of education and maturity to do their belated work. They *had* to do so: so much was at stake. And in the meantime, Bruce could continue supervising Bertie, hard though the task would be. The lessons would go on as well. It was no time to weaken.

However, Bertie was discovering his power—and also discovering how agreeable life could be. In Germany, at the age of seventeen, he had kissed a girl. It had been very brief, at a party in the country. Bertie had been slightly drunk, and there had been no chance for anything beyond this short embrace; even then, when the news leaked out, as it inevitably did, Gladstone had written to his wife about the Prince's "squalid little debauch." A few months later, on a short unofficial visit to New York, Bertie attended a ball in his honor and realized quite shrewdly just how interested women were in *him*. But it was really at Oxford that the great real revelation had occurred. In spite of General Bruce, in spite of Albert's fiat that "the only use of Oxford is that it is a place of *study*," Bertie had guardedly made contact with a few bold members of the wealthy Christ Church set.

There was young Henry Chaplin, appropriately nicknamed the "Magnifico." Worldly, flamboyant, and immensely rich, he represented everything Bertie's sheltered royal life had seemed to lack—wit, pleasure, gambling and horses, all of the easy arrogance of the English aristocrat. One of Magnifico's specialities was to turn up for college chapel wearing his regulation surplice over his well-cut hunting coat. Although no older than the Prince, he must have seemed the acme of sophistication, living luxuriously, eating and drinking splendidly (already something of a gourmet, he had his private chef at Oxford), and generally exhibiting the sort of stylishness that is so tempting at eighteen.

Chaplin was Bertie's first real encounter with the "unregenerate" eighteenth-century world of the English "Higher Classes" which his parents dreaded and opposed. He was predictably impressed but not, to his regret, seduced. "Governor" Bruce was there to see to that, although both Chaplin and another Christ Church rip and womanizer, Sir Frederick Johnstone, seem to have pointed out to Bertie the unrivaled opportunities that his position gave him. He could have any woman that he cared for—actress or married woman or member of society. Bertie apparently replied that things weren't quite that easy for a royal prince.

But one can see how from that very moment Albert's whole earnest system had finally lost out. Bertie had glimpsed his promised land and seen the sort of life he wanted. What earthly chance had Albert's system now against the lure of a lifetime's pleasure?

It was not until the final scandal at the Curragh that Albert knew for certain he had failed. It must have been a terrible defeat. Twelve years of unremitting effort to create Bishop Wilberforce's "most perfect man," Stockmar's advice and Ruskin's counsel, the day-to-day reports sent in by Gibbs, those early mornings working out the system by his student's lamp, all defeated by a common harlot. Perhaps one can understand Albert writing about "the greatest pain that I have yet felt in my life." In this respect at least, it was fortuitous that he died when he did, without ever learning the full truth about his system. For had it been the Devil, and not saintly Albert, who had devised Bertie's education, he could have hardly bettered the arrangements. Those years of forced application, boredom, restraint, and weary earnestness had been the perfect education for a royal rake. The Hanoverian instincts had been carefully enhanced by royal repression. Bertie the potential rake was ready. The only question now was how his rake's progress would begin—and when.

But Bertie

3

When Albert died, Lord Palmerston, a worldly man and something of a judge of character, warned Bertie feelingly against the "allurements of fortune, position and social temptation," which would soon be assailing him. This must have sounded hopeful to the Prince, but these "allurements" showed a depressing failure to materialize—Victoria saw to that.

Even the *Times*'s proposal that Bertie should assist his mother as an official welcomer and host for foreign diplomats and royalty came to nothing. Bertie must be shielded from temptation, and as Victoria wrote about herself and Albert, "she has had many conversations with her beloved angel and she feels that *she* knows exactly what he wished."

Probably she did. There was certainly no change in Bertie's situation. The reins had simply passed from Albert's hands to hers, and Bertie was still chafing in his harness. Even old Nanny Bruce remained his governor, reporting back his every mood and movement to eagle-eyed Mama. Grief had not softened her suspicious mind and Bertie was never one for fighting battles that he couldn't win—particularly with her.

It must have been a great relief for Bertie when he went off to Egypt. Albert himself had planned the trip as part of Bertie's further education. And by now the Prince had started on his life-long passion for travel: he enjoyed movement for the sake of moving. "Can *nobody* keep Bertie still?" Victoria was later to lament.

The Queen supervised the details and laid down the rules about the journey. Bertie was, of course, still to be carefully chaperoned—by Dean Stanley* now as well as by old General Bruce—and Victoria drove home the fact of his continuing dependence (although he was now past his majority) by issuing a set of truly Albertine instructions for the trip. Not merely was Bertie to be supervised *by night* as well as day; he was to read *improving* literature en route (sermons upon the Sabbath), he must be stopped from overeating, and on no account must he shoot on Sundays.

The Prince's attitude at this stage was anything for a quiet life. Nevertheless, as one reads of the actual events on the trip, one gets the feeling that he was becoming an adroit exponent of the pleasure principle, and seems to have enjoyed himself—despite the General and the Dean. He had boundless energy and a sense of fun (a remarkable achievement after a life at Windsor). The Sphinx reminded him of Bishop Wilberforce; he scrambled to the top of the Great

* Arthur Penrhyn Stanley (1815-81) was educated under Dr. Arnold at Rugby, and it was his life of the great educator, published in 1844, which did much to establish his legend among the Victorians. He was also a noted scholar of the Holy Land, a keen advocate of religious toleration, and a distinguished Dean of Westminster. His influence on Bertie originated with his wife, Lady Augusta, née Bruce, who was a close friend of Victoria.

Pyramid "with great alacrity" and when Said Pasha—much to Victoria's chagrin when she learned about it—spent £8,000 on entertaining him and organized a luxurious voyage along the Nile, Bertie accepted with the same alacrity with which he climbed the Pyramid. He obeyed the *spirit* of Mama's instructions by shooting only crocodiles on Sundays.

Egypt over, Bertie departed for the Holy Land, where he was soon traveling with unabated zest—Judaea, Jericho, the Dead Sea, Bethlehem—with the Dean tagging on, just "to impress the Prince with the sacredness of the associations." As a great favor, the authorities permitted Bertie to enter the mosque of Hebron—the first Christian to do so since 1187. As he stepped in he made the remark which could have been a motto for the remainder of his life. "High station," the Prince murmured, "has after all, some merits, some advantages."

It had indeed, and on the journey home, when he stopped off at Fontainebleau for a brief visit to Napoleon III, he saw some more of them. The Empress Eugénie had been married long enough to her outrageous husband to know a potential womanizer when she saw one, and summoned a bevy of attractive young ladies of the Court to meet the Prince of Wales. Bertie was still being scrupulously chaperoned. General Bruce had died on duty. (Blackwater fever and fatigue in Palestine —"a terrible blow . . . really too sad to think about.") But Sir Charles Phipps, Victoria's own Keeper of the Privy Purse, had been instantly dispatched to take his place: the Empress is supposed to have whispered to Sir Charles to overlook it if the Prince had just "one evening that is all pleasure and no duty."

Again this sounds more hopeful than it was. Even Napoleon III's court had certain limits; but the Prince evidently "danced and flirted" and met one woman who would later be his mistress, the tempestuous Princesse de Sagan, a banker's daughter who had just married the most famous dandy in Paris.

When news of all this reached the Queen, as reach the Queen it did, it must have settled one thing in her determined mind. Bertie must have a wife. It was his one remaining hope against a life of sin. Talk of his marrying had been in the air for more than a year, but Bertie had not appeared particularly enthusiastic.

This was quite understandable, for he was barely nineteen when his parents had first started worrying about his marriage. This was some time before his night with Nellie Clifden, so he was still completely inexperienced. Naturally they had not so much as considered the idea that Bertie should be left to sow his wild oats on his own and choose his bride himself. Bertie's marriage was too important to be left to Bertie. It must be arranged—like everything else in his life—by those who knew best and had his *real* interests at heart—i.e., his parents. They would find out what royal maidens were on offer in the courts of Europe, make the selection, and then finally Bertie would have the privilege of giving his assent—or not.

The task of finding the future Queen of England proved difficult. A commoner was unacceptable and suitable princesses in short supply. There was a Dutch princess but she, alas, was ugly: to have any chance at all, a bride of Bertie's must be beautiful. The best hope seemed to lie in Denmark, where there were royal granddaughters who were reported promising. With Victoria's approval the Queen's ambassador in Copenhagen was accordingly instructed to send photographs. The sixteen-year-old Alexandra appeared most attractive. But there were problems. Neither dynastically nor in terms of strict respectability was Danish royalty quite up to the mark. Moreover, a Danish connection would be a political liability to Britain—Prussia would resent it. Besides, the Princess's father was a mere captain in the Danish royal guard. The grandfather, the present king, was a disreputable old rip who had been thrice married and was not the sort of royalty Victoria approved of.

But there seemed no real alternative. Albert had been anxious to see Bertie married as soon as possible, and largely through his insistence a brief meeting had taken place between Bertie and Princess Alexandra at Speyer* in Germany during that eventful autumn of 1861. Despite the determined marriage plans of his parents, Bertie had been distinctly cool. According to his sister Vicky, who had chaperoned the Princess, "He had never seen a young lady who pleased him so much," but she added that "He was disappointed about her beauty and did not think her as pretty as he expected." After the meeting he had told his father that he would like to wait before he thought of marrying.

This seems to have puzzled and annoyed his parents, who were so used to arranging everything for Bertie. What they didn't know, of course, was that when he met Alexandra, he had just had his first experience of sexual freedom and full female beauty in Nellie Clifden. It was not too surprising that he was suddenly reluctant to tie himself prematurely to a wife—or that he had found this sixteen-year-old schoolgirl disappointing after the full-bodied charms of Nellie.

---

* Speyer, a small town on the west bank of the Rhine, became famous in the sixteenth century as the seat of the imperial diet, and six emperors were buried in its cathedral. It was chosen for the meeting because it was conveniently close to the Danish frontier and its sleepy picturesqueness hopefully gave an air of casualness to the encounter.

But even so, Albert had done his best to urge the Prince towards a speedy marriage. If he waited, Alix would, "in all probability, be the object of desire of other young princes," and more important still, Albert felt it was impossible for Bertie to lead a bachelor's life "with any chance of success or comfort to yourself." Bertie had tactfully agreed to differ.

Now, a year later, the question must have seemed more urgent still for Queen Victoria. From all that she had heard, Bertie seemed all too capable of leading a protracted bachelor's life with considerable success and comfort to himself. That was the danger and Victoria, in her self-appointed role as sole interpreter of her Beloved Angel's wishes, had convinced herself that all that Bertie needed was a wife.

How often have the parents of potential rakes convinced themselves that all the dear boy needed was a loving woman, children to care for, his own family to love. This was particularly so with Bertie. Victoria was no fool. She recognized the power of sin—and Bertie's susceptibility. "Poor Bertie," as she wrote about him later. "His is not a nature made to bear sorrow, or a life without amusement and excitement."

If he fell now, he could be lost forever. Think of the scandals, the excesses that would follow. Cumberland and Clarence and the old Prince Regent would have nothing on their great-nephew if he remained a bachelor. Then came a further worry—a rumor that the Tsar was on the prowl for a wife for the young Tsarevitch and had his eye on Alexandra. The question was becoming urgent. There could be no more wasting time. Bertie must marry without more ado.

As usual, when confronted with the maternal steamroller, Bertie submitted. It was all rather like the mating of valuable bloodstock—which in a sense it was—but once the arrangements had been settled, everyone became suitably romantic.

Victoria was quite aflutter, speaking of Alexandra's "beautiful refined profile and quiet ladylike manner." But there was
still one item on her conscience—"that dreadful business at
the Curragh." It couldn't be glossed over or forgotten—particularly as the Duke of Coburg, an opponent of the marriage,
was threatening to reveal all to the Danes. So, much to
Bertie's chagrin, Victoria insisted that Alexandra's parents
must be told "that *wicked wretches* had led our poor innocent boy into a scrape which caused his beloved father and
myself the deepest pain." Despite this, he had been forgiven, and the Queen was confident that he wanted nothing
more than domesticity and would make a "steady husband."

One fears that Victoria was confident of no such thing, but
honor at any rate was satisfied. This took place towards the
end of 1862. Victoria even arranged the spot where the proposal could take place—the grounds of her uncle Leopold
of the Belgians' palace of Laeken outside Brussels. Victoria,
traveling under the flimsy incognito of Countess Balmoral,
went there first to meet the Danish royal family and make
sure that everything was settled. (Bertie was plainly far too
unreliable to manage a proposal on his own.) Then and only
then was Bertie permitted to arrive, meet the Princess, and
pop the question. There was a note of resignation in his
remark to Lady Walburga Paget when the stage was set:
"Now I will take a walk with Princess Alix in the garden
and in three quarters of an hour I will take her into the
grotto and there I will propose, and I hope it will be to
everyone's satisfaction."

All this seems very different from the romantic letter
Bertie penned to his mama that same evening giving the joyous news of what had happened. "I cannot tell you with
what feelings my head is filled, and how happy I feel. I

only hope it may be for her happiness and that I may do my duty towards her. Love her and cherish her you may be sure I will to the end of my life."

Should one feel sorry for the Prince or was he learning fast to make the best of things? One must not be too cynical. After the frustrations of his adolescence, there was no reason for him not to have accepted the first princess he was permitted to pay court to. It was an "arranged" marriage, and his parents had left him little choice but to agree to it. But Alexandra was extremely pretty. She had considerable poise and sweetness. According to the Crown Princess, her beauty consisted in her grace and her expression, and it grew on one the more one saw her. It was plainly no hardship for anyone of Bertie's temperament to marry her.

She was patently if naïvely in love with him. "If he were a cowboy I would love him just the same and would marry no one else," she confided to Bertie's sister Vicky just before the marriage. Indeed, her girlishness struck everyone who met her. She seemed so artless, so uncomplicated and affectionate, the simple Danish maiden in a real-life fairy tale. Some thought her none too bright. Victoria—for whom she was immediately "dear, sweet Alix"—seems to have felt that she could twist her round her regal little finger. And certainly, as far as Bertie was concerned, he had found himself an utterly devoted bride in whose eyes he could do no wrong.

There were other less romantic advantages for him once he married her. One was financial. After discreet discussions with the Prime Minister and an arranged parliamentary vote, his future stipend was fixed at a regular £110,000 a year. He would also become entitled to a fitting residence in London. There were several royal properties to choose from, but Marlborough House had recently been renovated and was standing empty. It was central, comfortable, and imposing, with countless bedrooms, one of the loveliest ballrooms in London, adequate servants' quarters, stabling, a well-stocked cellar, and beautifully maintained gardens which adjoined the Mall. Whoever lived there could clearly play a key part in the social life of London.

Then there would have to be a country residence. This was more of a problem as there was nothing suitable belonging to the Crown. Large estates with splendid houses were hard to come by, but by the act of marrying, Bertie would have the right to call on capital accumulated for this purpose by his father. There was nearly half a million. It should be possible to find something fitting.

The year 1863 began with preparations for the wedding. Victoria seemed confident that "poor weak Bertie" had been taken care of in accordance with her Beloved Angel's wishes. The real question which the marriage raised was would Victoria be proved right and the love of his princess transform Bertie's life as Albert's love had once transformed hers?

The wedding, like the arrangements that led up to it, was dominated by Victoria. The Prince, and almost everybody else, had taken for granted that it would be held in London, either at the Abbey or St. Paul's. Victoria thought otherwise.

It was a full fifteen months since Albert had departed, but she insisted that a state procession through the capital was an ordeal which no one could expect a widowed queen to face. (The less generous suspected that she had no intention of sharing popular attention with a pretty young princess who might steal the limelight.) Instead, the Queen insisted on St. George's Chapel, Windsor. Bertie was still being held back from the center of the stage. In London his marriage would have been a state event; in Windsor it was very much a family affair.

Punch caught the point of this when it suggested sarcastically that since the wedding was being held "in an obscure Berkshire village, noted only for an old castle with no sanitary arrangements," the press should treat it all with great discretion. Publicity should be confined to a simple notice in the *Times* marriage column as follows—"On the 10th inst., at Windsor, by Dr. Longley, assisted by Dr. Thomson, Albert Edward England K.G. to Alexandra Denmark. No cards."

As it turned out, this was no bad suggestion, for the day was cold and blustery and the arrangements were chaotic. Disraeli had to sit on his wife's lap, the crowd got out of hand, and it was very clear that the ceremony had been insufficiently rehearsed. The carriages appeared "old and shabby, the horses very poor, with no trappings, not even rosettes, and no outriders."*

Victoria did little to improve the shining hour, apart from wearing the ribbon of the garter over her widow's weeds. Throughout the service she sat hidden in her private gallery, as if intent on shunning the entire proceedings, and afterwards she lunched with a solitary lady in waiting rather than face her son and newly acquired daughter-in-law. "What a sad and dismal ceremony it was!" she wrote afterwards with mournful satisfaction to the King of Prussia.

But Bertie rose to the occasion, showing his customary resilience and refusal to be depressed by his mother's grief. Clad in his garter robes and general's uniform he looked, wrote Clarendon, "very like a gentleman and more consider-

---

* Virginia Cowles (1973), from the diaries of James Howard Harris, Third Earl of Malmesbury—the distinguished Victorian diplomat and Foreign Secretary in Lord Derby's government.

able than he is wont to." Kindly Bishop Wilberforce, looking as usual on the bright side, pronounced the nuptials "the most moving ceremony I ever saw." And by general agreement, the Princess Alexandra was everything a royal bride should be: more than ever the fairy-tale princess in her silver dress.

The Eton schoolboys had a holiday, Tennyson penned some homespun lines, and bride and bridegroom finally steamed off aboard their special train to honeymoon at blessed Osborne, scene of so many blissful moments between Victoria and Albert during happier days.

The Rake's Apprenticeship

4

"Since God hath given us the Papacy," wrote Alexander VI, the Borgia Pope, on his election in 1492, "let us enjoy it!"

This, broadly speaking, was also the reaction of the Prince of Wales to his marriage on March 10, 1863. The moment he and his Princess moved in to Marlborough House at the start of April, the fun began—balls, dinners, celebrations, eating all night, and dancing till dawn. The Prince had never been so happy, nor the socialites of London; the social roundabout had lacked a center for so long; now it could turn again. And turn it did! The royal carnival had started. Faster and faster it continued as the first weeks of the London season started. May brought no slackening of pace and by June Disraeli was describing that year's season as an extended royal public honeymoon.

But it was more than just a honeymoon. For Bertie it must have seemed more like the celebration after years of exile. Repression and restraint were suddenly behind him. From

having been for years the most scrupulously guarded, supervised, fussed-over eminent young man in England, he had
been transformed overnight into the most sought-after, lavishly endowed, loved, and envied prince in Europe. It was a
fairy-tale beginning to his adult life—and as with all good
fairy tales it was a shade unreal. This was something London
had not seen for more than thirty years. The last time royalty
enjoyed itself in public was in the reign of George IV, and
he had been old and gouty. Bertie was young and vigorous,
his princess glamourous and beautiful, and they inevitably
became the rage of fashionable London.

This might have been expected. Certainly Victoria must
have had some inkling of what would happen after the
wedding. But she could have had no idea of the extent to
which her son would liberate himself—a liberation which in
her eyes soon became an unmitigated family disaster.

From the beginning there was a sour note of surprise in her
reactions to the freshly married couple. Just a few days after
their return from their honeymoon she was complaining that
his manners had definitely not improved. A few days more
and she launched forth on what was to be a standing complaint for the remainder of her life. Bertie was going out too
much. Bertie was frivolous. He and his wife were both looking distinctly ill from too much gadding around town. "Oh
how different poor foolish Bertie is to adored Papa, whose
gentle loving wise motherly care of me, when he was not 21,
exceeded everything."

But as the public honeymoon continued, and the Queen
began to catch the measure of what was really happening, she
changed from disappointment to alarm. At Marlborough
House a whole new era was beginning—just across the Mall
from Buckingham Palace—and there was nothing she could
do to stop it. Poor foolish Bertie, who was so unlike adored

Papa, had changed. Could this be the son that she and Albert had brought up so carefully, educated so sedulously for his moral calling as a leader of the nation? All that he did was to go out all night, mix with precisely that "bad set" of which his father disapproved, and wear out sweet Alix "till she will be a skeleton." This was all hideous enough, but worse still was the wider question—"What will become of the poor country when I die?"

The disillusioning of Queen Victoria is fascinating, for it went far beyond a simple failure on her part to take into account the celebrations and relief after the wedding. It involved a very real misunderstanding of Bertie's character. It would be going too far to say that he tricked her: perhaps it would be nearer the mark to say that she deceived herself. Certainly until his marriage Bertie had always been extremely cautious over how much he revealed of his true self to Mama. He played along with her sentimentality, paid lip service to her earnestness, and always slid out of a head-on battle on a point of principle. This was not surprising. Victoria was a powerful lady and Bertie in a very weak position. But all this led the Queen to make a fundamental error. He was so often "poor foolish Bertie" or simply "weak Bertie" that she failed to see his strength. And she also failed to take account of the extent of his reaction to his father's influence. Again, he generally disguised it or soft-pedaled it; but those years of tedium, the endless lessons and those moralizing talks, had brought an absolute rejection of the father image. Bertie was quietly but adamantly against almost everything that Albert stood for—his earnestness, his domesticity, his intellect. Where Albert was ascetic, Bertie was greedy; where he was stiff and formal, Bertie had ease and charm. Albert mistrusted people, dreaded immorality, and believed passionately in self-improvement. Bertie loved company, the louder the better, was sexually amoral, and believed passionately in one thing only—in enjoying himself.

With such divergence between son and father it was not surprising that Victoria should have misunderstood the Prince. Even so, it would have been a most perceptive mother who could have foreseen her son's behavior during these first frantic weeks of marriage. For Bertie did much more than wildly enjoy himself. One might have expected him simply to count his blessings and relax, then slowly learn what this new pleasant life could offer. Instead he knew exactly what he wanted, and during that first spring and summer of his marriage he was already working out the pattern of his life, a pattern which completed the rejection of his parents' wishes and formed the basis of the strange rake's progress which he pursued until the day he died.

For Bertie was a formal rake—punctilious, and careful and aware of his position, and he proceeded to exploit his status and prestige simply to ensure that life became as pleasant as he and his obliging friends could make it. In a sense this wasn't difficult. He and the Princess were in such demand that there was little people would not do for them. Society was eager to be at their disposal, fete them and feed them and do anything to please them. And he had his own resources now as Prince of Wales. Not long before his marriage he had spent £200,000 of his inheritance from Albert in purchasing a big estate at Sandringham in Norfolk; already he was busy spending more to make the house an ideal country residence, and to improve the shooting. More money went on making Marlborough House what it would soon become—the center of an alternative court in London from which the Prince would rapidly assume the royal social functions which

Victoria herself refused to shoulder. Apart from the social functions and ceremonial affairs he loved, Bertie had nothing to distract him.

Few people ever have the chance to make a life of total pleasure and of the few who do, still fewer manage to enjoy it. Bertie was the exception. Now that his marriage had freed him from Victoria's immediate control, the time had come to use his freedom. Bertie, to do him justice, made the most of it.

Ironically, much of the credit for this must go to his father. Held back so long from so many basic pleasures, there was no danger of boredom or world-weariness in Bertie and by making him the Philistine he was, Albert had perfectly adapted him to lead society. Had he turned out as Albert hoped, a sensitive and moral intellectual, Bertie's life would have become more difficult. What role could such a Prince of Wales have played? He would have been bored with polite conversation, still more frustrated by the Queen, and certainly depressed by the emptiness of his position.

Instead, Bertie possessed the perfect personality and appetites for his new situation. He wanted luxury and comfort and activity, amusing company, fast talk, rich food and pretty women and cigars. He enjoyed gambling and horses, shooting and hunting, and big country houses. There were other tastes as well which he still had to develop. As Prince of Wales, his pleasures and ambitions were absolutely matched by his possibilities; and as he planned his year, in the first springtime of his marriage, he did so with the rare decisiveness of someone who has carefully thought out what he wants in life and knows exactly how to get it.

In London he could instantly assume that leadership of smart society which Victoria had never wanted. This meant that from May to mid-July his life was crammed with a round of banquets, theatres, balls, receptions, garden parties. "The quality which most impressed contemporaries was the extraordinary energy displayed by the Prince as he rushed, day after day, from one social engagement to another. He could make do with little sleep; he liked his diary to show a crowded schedule and he hated to be kept waiting even for a moment."*

Even that first summer the Princess found some difficulty keeping up with all this avid socializing. Out of sheer self-defense she fell back on the stock device of shy and weary women—chronic unpunctuality. Bertie would complain about this all their married life.

From the start he made it clear that he was not letting her deflect him from what he naturally called his "social duties." Once she was pregnant—as she soon was—the way was plainly open for him to lead his own male energetic life; the pattern of their marriage was established. He ruled the roost.

Victoria's dreams of "dear, sweet Alix" as a restraining influence never had a chance. Alexandra was too simple-minded, too inexperienced and young to cope with rumbustious Bertie in that first flush of social triumph. She was late rising in the morning. Bertie was up and off. She missed her cozy family in Copenhagen, spoke English rather badly, and was touchingly dependent. Bertie quite clearly loved her in his way, was proud of her good looks, the way she dressed, the grace with which she filled her social role. Before long she would inevitably be an admirable mother. Bertie, the Prince of all male chauvinists in a male chauvinistic age, respected and treated her accordingly. Part of his life—a rather small part—was exclusively hers. No hint of disrespect would ever be permitted from his friends or mistresses at her ex-

---

* Sir Philip Magnus-Allcroft, *King Edward the Seventh.*

pense. She was above suspicion, above criticism—and rather above the Prince's ordinary life as well: a sort of female totem, smiling and regal and immaculate, gracing the Court of Albert, Prince of Wales.

In the meantime he was permitted—or, to be more exact, permitted himself—every male pleasure. He was the cynosure, the rakish dandy, dressing superbly, charming his regiment of new friends with his openness and bluff good nature, always available and wonderfully appreciative of every pastime which the rich could offer. For Goodwood week there was a small select house party in his honor with the Duke of Richmond. For Doncaster Races the Saviles entertained him and the Princess with a royal reception. At Ascot and Henley he was the guest of honor, then as July ended there was Cowes for yachting—another social triumph. He was the "sporting prince," admired and feted and energetically enjoying this effortless success.

During that first year of his marriage each of these events was entered upon the calendar which he adhered to for the remainder of his life. These social landmarks marked out the territory he ruled, race track and ballroom and large country house. Here he was sovereign, and offered a respect more absolute than any that the Queen received at Windsor.

People fell over themselves in patriotic zeal for the Prince, and his movements during the early summer took on the character of royal progresses. Before long the song "God Bless the Prince of Wales" was being lustily intoned whenever he appeared. But it was at Cowes that Bertie's social sovereignty was most apparent. In 1863, he was elected president of the Royal Yacht Squadron, an honor previously held by his father, and his enthusiastic presence in the Isle of Wight made Cowes week a truly royal occasion. This was the high point of the social season as the sailor prince raced in his cutter, *Dagmar,* and "sacred Cowes" became the center of the loyal cult devoted to yachting and the Prince of Wales.

After Cowes week he felt he needed to recover. Alix was sent off home to Copenhagen for a few weeks with her adoring family.* He infinitely preferred Paris for a few days on his own or, rather, in the contemporary phrase, *en garçon.* This was the normal thing for rich young married rakes to do in the 1860's. It was considered vaguely "good for them" to enjoy the pleasures of the city which would have been impossible when encumbered with a wife. Bertie, accompanied only by a few friends, could now enjoy this city he would always love.

Paris completed Bertie's liberation. Never before or since had the city experienced a decade quite like the sixties of the Second Empire, as the corrupt and glittering regime of Napoleon III led Paris in the final orgy that preceded the Franco-Prussian War of 1870. This was the golden age of the *grandes cocottes,* the *haute bicherie parisienne,* those pampered and stylish courtesans who dominated the smart life of Paris and who made it so different from the world of Queen Victoria. They were the city's principal celebrities, immensely wealthy with their own sumptuous establishments, women like the terrifying La Pavia, with her string of titled lovers and her great mansion, now the Travellers' Club, on the Champs Elysées; Blanche d'Artigny, the original of Zola's *Nana;* and Cora Pearl, the rock-hard "Pearl from

* The Prince found Copenhagen dull and was soon bored with the close family life of his in-laws which Alexandra adored. Only in moments of extreme guilt or family disaster would he willingly accompany her there. Normally she went alone.

Plymouth" who became the mistress of the Emperor—and of almost every member of the Jockey Club as well, including the Prince of Wales.

Their influence was enormous—particularly within the fashionable aristocratic world which feted Bertie. The Emperor, his old friend and mentor, was himself one of the most notorious rakes in Paris, a man who used his court rather like a brothel and who remarked that he needed a woman, like a good cigar, after every meal. It must have been interesting for the Prince that summer to find himself his guest.

Bertie spoke fluent French, had his own suite at the Hotel Bristol, and as the Earl of Chester seems to have enjoyed sufficient anonymity for his purposes. As the historian of the courtesans has written, "the very air of Paris seemed to encourage licence. Foreign celebrities passing through the capital hastened to pay their respects to the most notorious *filles en renom.*" The most famous of these, the actress Hortense Schneider, was apparently known as *le passage des princes,* a name which Bertie helped her earn by his assiduous attentions during his early visits to the capital.

It is not difficult to imagine the effect of such a world on Bertie—or to understand why that first summer-sampling of its pleasures was to be followed by three regular visits every year throughout the sixties. Here he could find what he had never known and what one never found in England—love treated as an art, a high society which pursued a civilized routine of sexual pleasure, a ready welcome from the most skillful mistresses in Europe. And Bertie possessed a nature to appreciate the contrast between all this and the simple pleasures of his schoolgirl bride.

After Paris—and by the sound of it none too soon at that—it was time for Bertie to move on to take the cure at one of the fashionable German spas. That first year, while the

Princess was still enjoying Copenhagen, he picked Wiesbaden. In later years he swung between Homburg and Baden-Baden and finally settled on Marienbad. But the routine would always be the same.

His social life continued. The daily calorific intake would subside; sitz baths and seltzer now in place of lobster and champagne, and Bertie's waistline would contract accordingly. But nothing could be further from the truth than to imagine that abstinence extended to his sex life. During the late summer season all of the fashionable German spas would suddenly become the hunting ground for the most famous courtesans of Europe, as smart society moved from Paris over the borders of the Rhine. In 1863 the notorious Blanche d'Artigny, like Bertie, was enjoying "the great annual exodus from Paris," at Wiesbaden. Along with her there was a regiment of lesser *filles de joie*, adventuresses of every age and dimension, and greater and lesser European nobility.

Far from these few weeks of the cure being a time of strict regime and clinical restraint, they were in fact another section of the social calendar. According to Marie Colombier, one of the well-known ladies of the period, "nothing can give any idea of the first fortnight in September at Baden-Baden during the sixties. . . . It was the fantasy, the irresponsible madness of the *kermesses* of olden times."*

There would be operas and concerts and entertainments. Much gambling took place, and once again Bertie, with his energy and appetites and social genius, found himself entirely at home. This was emphatically no place for Alexandra, and he was very much the bachelor prince, conversing naturally in French or German, gambling, conducting his incidental affairs and hobnobbing, as his first biographer describes him, with "Russian Grand Dukes and Duchesses,

* Joanna Richardson, *The Courtesans.*

Austrian Archdukes and Archduchesses, minor German princes and princesses and the old nobility of France."*

This was in fact another role for him to play—and one which he enjoyed for the remainder of his life. His character was forming rapidly, and he was now becoming something more than the straightforward English gentleman Albert had tried to make him. His ancestry had started to assert itself; he was very much the gilded cosmopolitan royal rake.

On his way back from Germany he enjoyed a few last days in Paris before meeting the Princess and returning to England for the autumn. It would be time then for another Bertie to take over—the kindly husband and the country-loving Englishman—as they steamed up to Sandringham, then on to Scotland to shoot grouse before the winter. Like many happily unfaithful husbands, he was at his most devoted after he had been away, and always insisted that they spend his birthday—November—back at Sandringham. This was the opening of Bertie's family season—a large birthday party on the ninth with his relatives and close friends invited, lavish entertaining for the local gentry, and Christmas always a cheerful family affair, complete with an enormous tree for the Sandringham dependents and a great table stacked with presents for the family and friends. Bertie would play the paterfamilias with gusto. There would be balls and parties, and it was now that the Princess, with her passion for her children and for practical jokes and dancing, came into her own. She made the most of it, for by February Bertie would already be showing signs of restlessness.

At Sandringham and Marlborough House, Bertie ignored convention by seeming to invite anyone who interested him. The circle of his friendships was to grow extremely wide. After the strict formality and stuffiness of Victoria's court,

* Sir Sidney Lee, *King Edward VII: A Biography.*

this in itself seemed revolutionary. Victoria naturally disapproved, but later Bertie was to be almost universally praised for his lack of snobbery, his open-mindedness against outmoded class distinctions and his extraordinary eagerness to include Jews, jockeys, businessmen, and even foreigners in his confidence.

All this is true. Bertie had catholic tastes in male as well as female friends, and his behavior helped extend the popularity of monarchy—as well as the range of royal influence and interests. But he was emphatically no democrat, and paradoxically the pleasure-seeking months after his marriage saw him becoming more firmly wedded to the tastes and interests of the aristocracy than his mother ever had been. She had brought him up to distrust the "Higher Classes," but once he was free to please himself he soon became one of them by self-appointment and adoption. For, despite his apparent unconcern with class distinctions, it was the aristocracy alone who could satisfy his love of pleasure and give him what he wanted out of life.

The London season was still their exclusive domain. They owned the enormous country houses where Bertie loved to be received and fed and feted on the grandest scale. They had the hunting, and more important still, the large-scale shooting that he so enjoyed. They had the acreage and wealth that could support him in his role as country-loving "sportsman," while the richest of them, magnates like Hartington and Sutherland and Richmond, could afford what Bertie at the moment couldn't—patronage of the turf, "the sport of the kings."

All of this naturally bound the pleasure-loving Prince of Wales to the nobility, but there was more to it than that. From the moment when he had met members of the rich, rakish set at Oxford—young bloods like Hastings, Chaplin, and the womanizing baronet Sir Frederick Johnstone—Bertie had tacitly adopted much of their attitude. They had so much more glamour and excitement than those earnest middle classes on whom his parents pinned their hopes for the country's future. Here in the sixties they still managed to preserve much of the carefree rakishness of the Regency, and Bertie, beginning his discreet revolt against his father, emotionally adopted them.

This was what Queen Victoria had feared, and this was what really lay behind her constant admonitions against his interest in the "Higher Classes" and the bad company he kept. This was betraying everything that Albert stood for. Bertie had gone over to the enemy, but there wasn't much that she could do about it.

Bertie's defection would have far-reaching implications in the years ahead, and already his concern with pleasure and the social life was being seen as a setback to the great cause of earnestness and virtue. Even in the first weeks of his marriage when the Prince, "initiating his long career of country-house host," had invited a collection of his aristocratic friends to Sandringham, Victoria had been suspicious. Lord Granville had sent her an enthusiastic report of his stay, innocently imagining that she would be pleased to hear about it, but she sourly replied that social pleasure was consuming an excessive share of his attentions. But at that time she still "sought consolation in the rather delusive hope that a study of serious books 'will gradually follow.' "

Of course it never did. Bertie, as one of his close friends remarked, was congenitally incapable of concentrating on a single thing for more than half an hour at a stretch. Reading a newspaper was an effort, a book a complete impossibility.

While he never made any pretense of intellectual interests,

or tried to hide his own allegiance to the "smart set" of society, there was one area in which he was discreet—the undercover rake's life which he was soon enjoying with his wilder friends in London. This was a very different world of pleasure from the sophisticated demimonde of Paris, but he enjoyed it just as much. He was a rake of truly catholic tastes and as prepared to sleep with a fashionable harlot as a duchess.

London continued the old eighteenth-century tradition by which it was accepted that young bloods of the nobility pursued their pleasures in the elaborately dissolute night life of the city. The range and the depravity of London's low life in the sixties were still notorious: all tastes were catered to and every imaginable form of vice an offer. There was little grace or finesse about this aspect of the city. Hardened foreigners could still be shocked by the sight of Haymarket thronged with its nightly company of streetwalkers; Leicester Square with its drinking dens and brothels outdid anywhere in Europe for sheer squalor; Spitalfields still had its notorious child brothels, while Mayfair and parts of Chelsea catered extravagantly to the carriage trade in vice.

One of the conventions was that wealthy rakes could sample the pleasures of the city in relative safety, and some of these places reached the height of fashion. Mott's Dancing Rooms in Foley Street, for instance, was a unique institution, ruled with immense propriety by its white-waistcoated owner, Freer, who prided himself on the distinction of his clientele. Parvenus were turned away, young nobles treated with due deference—"Really, my Lord, these practical jokes just cannot be permitted," Freer would exclaim—and he always prided himself on the deportment and beauty and discretion of the ladies.

Most of the famous beauties of the town were to be seen here in their day, ready to be bought champagne and listen to the "half dozen seedy instrumentalists who sat in the orchestra loft above the ballroom"—"Skittles" from Liverpool, the favorite mistress of the Earl of Hartington, "Sweet Nellie" Fowler, so called for the natural perfume that her skin exuded, "Shoes," "who eventually became Lady ——," and even Bertie's first love, Nellie Clifden.

A rival establishment was Cremorne Gardens in Chelsea. This was bigger and far less exclusive, but in summer it would be a great place for assignations and for the young bucks and the ladies of the town who could mingle here with the crowd of roisterers and cockneys enjoying a good night out. It was mild, racy, democratic. One could dance, listen to the orchestra, make love in the "Hermit's Cave" or the "Fairy Bower," have dinner with one's mistress in a private box, or have one's pocket picked in the crowd on Derby night.

During this period before photography had made Bertie's face the best-known physiognomy in Europe, he could still wander incognito with his friends about the capital. After the purdah-like existence he had led until his marriage, this sort of freedom must have seemed an untold luxury, and Bertie never tired of it. One of his simplest pleasures was to be driven quite anonymously in an ordinary cab. Another was to don old clothes and, accompanied by Lord Hartington and the Duchess of Manchester, dash off to see a fire.*

It hardly mattered that he was having to sow his wild oats *after* his marriage rather than before. Alexandra knew her place—and presumably had more sense than to ask too many

* At one stage Captain Eyre Shaw, the head of the London Fire Brigade, had orders to report a good blaze immediately to Marlborough House.

questions. And Bertie had the benefit of some of the best-informed guides to London's low life among his aristocratic friends. The sage Lord Hartington—for all his vast wealth, dignity, and growing political distinction—was a wide-ranging womanizer who combined a wild infatuation with Skittles and a twenty-year affair with the married Duchess of Manchester with countless transient amours. Sir Frederick Johnstone, a constant visitor to Marlborough House and Sandringham, had a reputation as an outstanding lecher, profligate, and drunk. The elegant young lords Dupplin and Hardwicke were both eager ladies' men, and during this period "wildness" was so much the accepted thing among the young bloods around the Prince that his own behavior must have appeared quite unremarkable.

If there was any single person who helped corrupt the Prince it was the twenty-three-year-old Marquis of Hastings, who was his earliest guide to the low life of the city. Absurdly rich and even more absurdly irresponsible, he really could have been as dangerous an influence on Bertie as Queen Victoria, who thoroughly disliked him, feared. For Hastings was the sort of self-annihilating rake who had flourished around the Earl of Rochester during the Restoration. Everything about him was extreme—his good looks, his wealth, his gambling, and his love of violence. His passion for low life and criminals made him at home in the brothels and the sailors' dives of Rotherhithe. His unconcern for money led him to squander his huge fortune on lunatic bets and overpriced and broken horses. He was a favorite companion of the Prince when he went to Mott's and the Cremorne, but even here he was a well-known hell-raiser. "Beg pardon, my lord, no larks tonight," Freer would say anxiously when he appeared. For it was at Mott's that Hastings had perpetrated his most famous and most typical practical joke, paying Richardson the rat-catcher twenty guineas to produce two hundred full-grown sewer rats tied up in sacks.

When the dancing was at its height, one of Hastings's friends turned out the lights and Hastings released the rats. Since Hastings was a Marquis old Freer had naturally forgiven him—and the affair had made his name as one of the liveliest blades in London.

Such a man instantly appealed to Bertie, for Bertie had always loved practical jokers ever since Albert had so specifically forbidden them—and Hastings could lead him to a world which none but the wildest rakes could know. Cockfighting was illegal, but at Faultless's Pit in Endell Street, the Marquis would match his birds against the Duke of Hamilton's. He was a keen patron of "ratting matches," where the nobility would bet on how many sewer rats a terrier could kill within the hour. He could show him the low life of the docks, and lead him through the night haunts of St. Giles Circus, where "the wild Markis" was a well-known figure.

One will never know whether it was luck, or something of his natural discretion, that preserved the Prince from being caught out in the sort of scrapes his friends involved him in. From time to time there would be rumors of the wild life he was leading. Occasionally a disreputable magazine like the notorious *Tomahawk* would hint at what was going on. Apart from this the Prince completed his rake's apprenticeship in the wild London of the sixties without an open scandal—which, considering his vulnerability, was something of an achievement. One can do nothing but admire the ruthlessness and gusto with which the royal heir continued to pursue the iron round of pleasure which he had made his life. Nothing diverted him, neither his wife, nor his mother, nor the fear of antagonizing the earnest middle classes. Bertie was a royal rake of genius. No one else has ever managed to combine such self-indulgence and so many fleshly pleasures with such a round of "social duties" and such regal gallivanting as Albert Edward, Prince of Wales, during these first years of his marriage.

Rake
in Trouble

5

It was too much to hope that Bertie's existing mode of life could go on for ever, although he seemed to act as if it would. Indeed, his cheerful carelessness, his ease and informality were striking during the years just following his marriage. How very enviable his life appeared, and how wholeheartedly he seemed to be enjoying it.

True he was gluttonous, a lecher and a Philistine. True also that he kept bad company, laughed at quite dreadful jokes, sponged on his wealthier friends, and chased after women of the town. But at least he made no pretense of being other than he was. Undoubtedly extremely popular among his friends, who all remarked upon his kindliness and loyalty, he was beginning to be spoken of as "handsome" and a "swell"—even, the ultimate accolade of rakishness, a "heavy swell." He was very much in tune with that section of society he loved, doing exactly what was expected of him —and just occasionally slightly more.

His wealthy friends all loved to be exploited by him—and only begged for more. His wild friends did nobody much harm—except themselves. Husbands whose wives he slept with felt it an honor to be cuckolded by him, while the ladies of the town all spoke of him most tenderly and claimed to have enjoyed his favors, whether they had or not.

Certainly he seemed to have the knack of keeping everyone as happy as himself. At Marlborough House he was the perfect host, fashionable, solicitous, and rarely known to forget a face—particularly a pretty one. At Sandringham, clad in his well-cut tweeds, he was the ideal country squire, hunting enthusiastically, shooting inordinately, and weighing his guests before they left to see if they had benefited from the *cuisine.* He spent heavily on the house and the estate. The amount of game slaughtered each year on his land rose from 7,000 to 30,000, which was considered laudable; and Sandringham became the extremely comfortable, much-loved home of Alexandra and their ever-growing family.* With his children he was a doting father, quite the antithesis of Albert—tolerant, humane, and undemanding. Despite Victoria's occasional concern to keep them from "contamination by the society in which their parents delighted," the royal brood was flourishing, apparently quite free from moral taint. The Princess was a dedicated mother, soon to become the "Dearest Mother-dear" of all her children, and Bertie was to manage the achievement almost unknown with English royalty of staying on lifelong good terms with all his offspring.

The truth was that Bertie was a supreme compartmental-

---

* Their five children were: Albert Victor, Duke of Clarence (1864–92), George, Duke of York and future King George V (1865–1936), Louise Victoria, Princess Royal (1867–1931), Victoria (1868–1935), and Maud (1869–1938).

izer, and during this charmed period seemed to have found a way of keeping each separate area in order, and more or less content—all except one, the Queen.

Throughout this period she kept up a discordant dirge at him from Windsor, about his life, his friends, and the example that he set. Even poor dear Alix was not immune. She was not making Bertie's home as comfortable as Victoria had hoped, and the Queen terribly disapproved of her unpunctuality and the late hour at which she breakfasted. But the main blasts from Windsor were directed against Bertie and "Society." As early as 1863 she was trying to insist that the Wales's "should not go out to dinners and parties during the London season, and that their social lives must be restricted to occasional visits to the houses of two or three high-ranking Cabinet ministers—Lord Granville, Lord Palmerston, and possibly Lord Derby" and to a few great houses like "Apsley, Grosvenor and Spencer Houses—but not," the Queen added cautiously, *"all* these the *same* year."

As well might Victoria have seriously proposed that Bertie give up eating. Even so he did his best to humor her. Invariably polite, and quite conciliatory, he never really let her strictures stop him from doing what he wanted. He knew better than to argue except on the rarest of occasions, such as when she suggested that he should restrict his days at Ascot. This was serious. Gently but firmly Bertie refused any curtailment of his racing. As he explained, his friends would be disappointed if he failed to turn up at Ascot. Worse still, people would wonder what was going on. "I am always most anxious to meet your wishes, dear Mama, in every respect, and I always regret if we are not quite *d'accord*—but as I am past twenty-eight and have some considerable knowledge of the world and society, you will, I am sure, at least

I trust, allow me to use my own discretion in matters of this kind. . . ."

Bertie was getting bolder. A few years earlier it would have been unthinkable for him to have used quite such directness to the Queen, but as the sixties ended certain events began impinging on the Prince's growing confidence. The carefree days were evidently over and it began to seem that Bertie's rakish life could never be the same again.

First there was trouble with the press, not very serious trouble, but enough to sound a note of caution. During his earliest days of freedom he had been able to adopt a breezily high-handed attitude towards reporters. Lee quotes a letter which he wrote from Sandringham in 1862. "Fancy on Saturday last a reporter from Lynn actually joined the beaters while we were shooting, but as I very nearly shot him in the legs as a rabbit was passing, he very soon gave me a wide berth. Gen. Knollys then informed him that his presence was not required, and he 'skidaddled' as the Yankees call it. The next day he wrote an apology for his infamous conduct, and I don't think he will trouble us any more."*

But it was no longer quite enough to inform the press that their presence was not required. They, too, were becoming just a little bolder. Compared with the century before—and the century to come—the press of the mid-Victorians possessed a matronly sense of what was dignified and proper. It was emphatically not an age of cheap scurrility. There was no investigative reporting and of course no instant press photography to intrude upon the private lives of the notorious and great. But even so, Bertie's behavior was becoming news, and ominously it appeared that items could leak out. Bertie's immunity was almost over.

* Sir Sidney Lee, *King Edward VII: A Biography.*

The first real warning came when the *Times,* for reasons of its own, picked up the rumors and reports from France about the Prince's "friendship" with Hortense Schneider. She was but one of many actresses Bertie paid court to during those weeks *en garçon* in Paris and on the Riviera, and normally he could count on Paris gossip not to cross the Channel. Certainly he had been indiscreet, visiting behind the scenes at the theatre, calling at her house, and dining with her several nights in succession. She knew the value of the publicity of having such a famous lover, and clearly made the most of it. But when the *Times* of London chose to print such stories it would not be long before the press began looking for its gossip slightly nearer home. It was a dangerous precedent for that carefree private life to hit the newspapers, particularly with things starting to go wrong.

Victoria had never liked the Hastings family. As an extremely young Queen she had suffered infinite embarrassment over the rumored pregnancy of her mother's lady in waiting, the unmarried Lady Flora Hastings. In the event poor Lady Flora, far from being pregnant, proved on examination to be a virgin suffering from a painfully enlarged liver. The Hastings family had been somewhat less than understanding over the whole affair, and the Queen had heartily disliked them ever since. Inevitably her "jobations" against Bertie's low companions mentioned young Henry Hastings. And now, as if to prove her right, the Marquis started to commit the one sin Bertie could not tolerate—he began a public scandal. Worse still, it was a scandal that involved another close friend of the Prince's, Henry Chaplin, the Magnifico himself. It was all most unfortunate, particularly as the whole thing started with just the sort of jape that Bertie loved.

Chaplin had never been a dedicated womanizer of the class of Hastings or Sir Frederick Johnstone or the Prince of Wales. Like many English gentlemen, he preferred horses. He felt that hunting was manlier than whoring, and his taste in women verged on respectability. He preferred hunt-balls to brothels and it was very much in character when he became engaged to one of the most admired beauties of the day, the young and shapely Lady Paget, known familiary as "the pocket Venus."

For Hastings this presented something of a challenge. Chaplin would have to be shown up. It was a chance to score off a rival, and he planned it rather as he planned the practical jokes that Bertie so enjoyed. Quite how he did it is a mystery. Perhaps Lady Paget was already slightly bored with her *fiancé's* passion for the turf, perhaps she found the rakish Hastings irresistible. Whatever happened, Hastings managed to make Chaplin look a fool in one of the most publicized stunts of the sixties. Chaplin was completely unsuspecting on the morning that he took Lady Paget shopping in Knightsbridge. They went to Marshall and Snelgrove's, and while Chaplin dutifully waited for his lady at the front entrance, she gave him the slip. At a side door, Hastings was waiting with a cab and a marriage license, and by lunchtime Chaplin has lost his pocket Venus, while Hastings had gained a wife.

For Hastings, whose sense of humor was rather special, the whole thing really was a joke, and if it had all occurred in private, no one would have laughed louder than the Prince. But Bertie was beginning to appreciate the important difference between private fun and public scandal. The Queen was outraged—so was the great moral middle class—and suddenly the entertainment value of the Marquis seemed dubious, particularly when the joke became a feud between Hastings and his deeply wounded rival. Indeed it turned out something of a classic of the period. In France it would undoubtedly have ended in a duel. Bertie's pacific presence managed to prevent that, but he could not stop the two men's hatred—nor could he stave off the fate which now marked down his friend and former fellow rake. For Hastings, in true style of self-destructive rakishness, was hell-bent on disaster, while Chaplin, careful and dignified as ever, was to achieve spectacular revenge.

The climax, when it came, was cast in the tradition of high Victorian melodrama. Chaplin's horse, Hermit, was entered for the Derby, and shortly before the race had burst a blood vessel in the neck. A rumor started that the horse had hemorrhaged, the odds against him rose dramatically, and for a while it seemed that Chaplin would scratch him from the race. This he refused to do. Instead he backed him heavily, while Hastings bet as heavily against him, so that two fortunes rested on his failure or success.

Bertie was in the Royal Box to see the race, and significantly it was Chaplin, not Hastings, who was in his party. By now everybody knew the state of the betting and what was at stake. Chaplin had refused to have his horse's coat cut since there was sleet and snow. Some of the people in the enclosure laughed when the horse appeared and the odds against him rose to sixty-six to one.

The race proved one of the most exciting in the history of the Derby, with Hermit winning by a neck. Chaplin won £140,000. Hastings lost just about as much, which ruined him financially. By now he was consumptive, and his losses seem to have made his condition worse. It would be nice to think that Hastings found some consolation in his pocket Venus, but he was a rake, not a romantic. The joke had gone against him, life had turned very sour. Within a year he died, worn out, embittered, bankrupt. His last words were reputedly— "Hermit's Derby broke my heart, but I didn't show it, did I?" Bertie did not go to the funeral; but he presumably read the *Times* obituary of his former friend. It was perhaps unnecessarily harsh, talking about peers of high rank who drag their dignity in the dirt. It was a warning Bertie was quite ready to take to heart.

Other straws were in the wind, suggesting that the carefree times were over. Money was not so plentiful, even among the greatest landowners who in the sixties had been reaping effortless fortunes from their vast estates. Now that the price of wheat was falling, people were pausing before they squandered their thousands—even in the Prince's honor. Another old friend and founder-member of the Wales's circle, Lord Hardwicke, immortalized as the inventor of the top hat, was also to go bankrupt—partly, at least, from the expense of the Prince's friendship. And Bertie himself began to feel the pinch. The £100,000 voted him each year by Parliament never would reach quite far enough. True, he was *not* all that extravagant, whatever people said about him. His gambling debts were not exorbitant, and he was never all that generous, even with his women. The contact with the princely form was generally taken—at any rate by Bertie —as its own unparalleled reward. There might be some little souvenir: a signed photograph, a monogrammed cigarette case. But there were no lavish showers of jewels on grasping mistresses—still less would Bertie ever have behaved as his much richer friend Lord Hartington did when he ended his liaison with the lovely Skittles,* setting her up in Mayfair with splendid house and gilt-edged annuities. With women, as with friends, the Prince lived—as they say of armies—off the country.

But even so, the life he lived could not be managed on a shoestring. The eating and the gallivanting all cost money— so did the clothes, the servants, and those wretched birds slaughtered in their thousands out at Sandringham. Bertie was never one to stint himself. He was a prince—and very conscious of the outward show of princely dignity. Moving among the very rich, he had much keeping-up to do. His carriages, his yacht, the butlers, valets, servants, secretaries, were a devouring expense which never could be completely covered by his parliamentary grant. During the first years of his marriage he quite cheerfully made up the difference out of capital—nearly half a million left him by his frugal father. Sandringham had taken quite a chunk of this. Now the remainder was nearly gone.

He did try certain small economies. In 1869 he saved a useful £2,000 a year by selling the Sandringham foxhounds. That same year in Paris he found moneylenders outside his hotel. Word had got round about his difficulties and the future King of England was considered a sound economic risk.

But Bertie saw no reason why he should get into debt. He always made a great point of speaking of himself as some-

* Hartington was only one of the many lovers of the most famous and spectacular *demi-mondaine* of the sixties. Born Catherine Walters, the daughter of a Liverpool sea captain, she earned her nickname during an argument with some drunken Guards officers whom she threatened to knock down like "a row of bloody skittles." Apart from her beauty and her rich clientele she was famous for the immaculate turn-out of her victoria and its high-stepping ponies, with which she drove every afternoon in the park.

thing of a social martyr. The dinners that he loved, the long weekends, and the receptions were all his social duties, and he felt quite strongly that he ought to be paid properly to do them. For once, Victoria agreed with him, and in the spring of 1869 was telling the Prime Minister that her son "hoped," nay more, "expected" Parliament to vote him a larger income. Gladstone quite adamantly shook his head.

For Bertie this in itself was bad enough, but this refusal was a symptom of something far more worrying—a hardening of feeling now against the monarchy. Republican feeling was reviving—partly due to wider social unrest, partly to a sense of grievance at a queen who spent her days in purdah-like retirement at Windsor, and partly to middle-class disapproval of Bertie's rakishness. For the first time Bertie was beginning to receive unfavorable publicity. Press cartoons showed him as a man of pleasure, and in the same year an unknown author published a satire called *The Coming K– – –*. Taking Tennyson's *Idylls of the King** as its unlikely model, it portrayed an unmistakable Bertie, surrounded by his pleasure-seeking courtiers (the "Dinner-table knights") avidly pursuing all the low life of the town. The author, who in fact

---

* Tennyson's *Idylls of the King,* which the Poet Laureate wrote between 1842 and 1885, formed a useful basis for the satire, portraying as they did the high hopes that attended King Arthur's coming and the gathering disillusionment with the Court and his followers. Great offense was caused when the author of *The Coming K– – –* turned from castigating Bertie and his friends, and started to reprove Victoria herself.

> "Surely would sing all England a Te Deum
> If she could her beloved Queen persuade
> To lock for once and all the Mausoleum,
> And leave, in peace, the dear departed shade;
> Be less the *egoiste,* think less of *'meum',*
> Save hard-worked ministers, and commerce aid,
> By ending her seclusion;—and to lean,
> Being still a woman, to be more a Queen!"

was A. A. Dowty of the Paymaster General's Office, possessed considerable inside knowledge, much of which he now made public. The Duchess of Manchester became "the Dame of Cottonopolis," Bertie was "Cuelpho." He was described watching a red-nosed comic in a music hall, visiting actresses in Leicester Square, and sampling the night life of the Haymarket. Bertie had been immune to public interest for too long. Now he was suddenly exposed as something of a butt to public ridicule. The tiresome warnings of the Queen about his low companions and the life he led were proving right. No wonder that poor Bertie nearly lost his nerve when real disaster burst on his now balding head one January day in 1870.

Bertie had known Harriet Moncrieffe almost since childhood. Her parents were near neighbors at Balmoral and favorites of the Queen. One of her sisters, who became Duchess of Athlone, was made lady in waiting at the court, and Harriet, who was something of a beauty, had remained an occasional friend of both the Waleses. She was entertained at Marlborough House and after her marriage to Sir Charles Mordaunt she and her husband had been to the theatre with Bertie and Alexandra.

As far as anybody knew, that was the extent of the relationship. One can imagine Bertie's feelings when he was informed that Mordaunt was suing his young wife for divorce. The two co-respondents named were both important members of the Prince's set: Lord Cole and Bertie's womanizing friend from Christ Church, Oxford, Sir Frederick Johnstone. This in itself was bad enough. There had been quite sufficient gossip about Bertie's circle lately, and he was developing strong views against what he called "public laundering"— the upper classes "washing their dirty linen in public." Mor-

daunt, although a rich conservative M.P., was clearly something of a traitor to his class, and the divorce could only lead
to trouble for the Royal Family. Mordaunt should obviously
have known better.

But there was worse to come—much worse—and just a
few days later Bertie was writing to his mother giving the
ghastly news. "It is my painful duty to inform you that I have
been 'sub-poenaed' by Sir C. Mordaunt's counsel to appear as
a witness on Saturday next at Lord Penzance's court." And
who knew what would happen then?

The truth, as Bertie knew quite well, was that he was in an
extremely vulnerable position. Mordaunt had not quite had
the temerity to name the Prince as co-respondent. But even
so, no Prince of Wales had ever before been subpoenaed to
appear in one of his parent's courts of law: if he were
harshly questioned then by Mordaunt's counsel, there could
be dreadful revelations. For Bertie's relations with the lady
had been extremely indiscreet. He was in what he would probably have called "a very nasty scrape," and much would now
depend on how the case was handled in the court.

In fact, the story of the Prince and Lady Mordaunt is one
of the few occasions when the bedroom farce of Bertie's
private life turned into tragicomedy. For after her marriage
to her rich, pigeon-shooting, M.P. husband, she had become
increasingly involved with Bertie and his circle. Just for a
while she must have seemed the perfect married woman for
their purposes—eager, promiscuous, and obviously already
bored with her husband. His concern with politics and
pigeon-shooting left her with time for her affairs, and unlike
most of the married women willing to sleep around, she was
still very young and rather beautiful. This, as it happened,
was half the trouble: the Mordaunts had not reached the
stage of casual indifference to each other's infidelities that

formed the basis of so much Victorian adultery. Mordaunt was still in love with his young wife, while she still lacked that asbestos lining to the sensibilities that was so necessary for any woman playing sexual hide-and-seek around the Prince.

For more than a year, during 1867 and 1868, Bertie had been close to her, visiting her house several times a week, writing her notes—those very noncommittal notes he already had the sense to write to married women—and even sending her a Valentine. Then the relationship had tapered off, as friendships between women and the Prince all tended to with time, and Johnstone and Lord Cole took over.

The crisis came towards the end of 1869. Lady Mordaunt had by now given birth to a child. The child was nearly blind. The mother, ill after the confinement, was overcome with wretchedness and guilt and seems to have suffered some sort of nervous breakdown. According to the evidence given in court, she called her husband and confessed that the child's father was Lord Cole; her wickedness was the cause of the baby's blindness. Sir Charles asked her what she meant, and she said she had "done very wrong . . . with Lord Cole, Sir Frederick Johnstone, the Prince of Wales and others, often, and in open day."

The proper and accepted course for a gentleman in such a situation was to have kept the skeleton firmly in the cupboard. He could have left his wife and shot more pigeons or taken any consolation that he wished; but appearances should have been maintained, while simple patriotism demanded that Bertie's good name be defended at all costs. But Mordaunt was no gentleman—nor, by the standards of the day, can he have been particularly loyal. Perhaps he was even human enough to want revenge—on Bertie and the cynical young rakes around him. This was extremely dangerous, for such a mood could find an echo in the now-suspicious minds of the great moral middle class. They had already been alerted to the Prince's pleasures. Now in the February days of 1870, there was a whiff of outrage in the air.

As Bertie's official biographer put it with masterful blandness, "The irresponsible gossip spread a misconception of the Prince as a superman of pleasure, who lacked serious interests. From time to time, public opinion was unsettled by the allegation."*

Now that the crisis she had always feared had come, it was Victoria who showed her mettle. Not for nothing was she Queen of England! Few parents could have acted quite so coolly to protect their erring offspring as Victoria did now. There was no time for recrimination, nor even for the faintest doubt about the dear boy's innocence. Bertie might be most injudicious in his friendships. She had said so many times. But he was also the repository of the English monarchy and any threat to that must immediately be dealt with.

It was too late to hush the whole thing up. Bertie was clearly going to have to go through with it, but there was still a great deal that the Queen could do—and did. First there was a letter to Bertie, to calm him down and make it plain that she was with him: she expressed her faith in him and simply asked him to be more circumspect in future. Bertie remained shaken and distinctly penitent—plainly frightened of the ordeal ahead. Her next move was to contact the Lord Chancellor just to make sure that nothing "untoward" occurred in court: and he, in his turn, arranged with Lord Penzance to shield the Prince in court, "should any improper questions be put by the Mordaunt counsel," as he put it in a note to the Queen.

* Sir Sidney Lee, *King Edward VII: A Biography.*

Victoria's chief concern, as usual, was the effect the trial would have upon the Prince's image. As she wrote to the Lord Chancellor, "the fact of the Prince of Wales's intimate acquaintance with a young married woman being publicly proclaimed will show an amount of imprudence which cannot but damage him in the eyes of the middle and lower classes, which is most deeply to be lamented in these days when the higher classes, in their frivolous, selfish and pleasure-seeking lives, do more to increase the spirit of democracy than anything else."

There was one more attempt to divert the scandal—by the loyal Sir Thomas Moncrieffe, the lady's father, who somewhat ruthlessly but patriotically had his daughter promptly declared insane. Leading doctors entered court to swear that she had been afflicted by "puerperal mania" after the birth of the child. This was accepted by the judge; Mordaunt's demand for a divorce would have to wait, but he still insisted that the court consider whether or not his wife's confession to him had been genuine. Bertie's appearance in the court was still demanded.

He must have had some sleepless nights. Would Mordaunt's counsel twist his answers under cross-examination? Would he be finally caught out? "I am in a very awkward position, and you can easily imagine how I am worried, dearest Mama," he wrote.

He need not have been. The Queen, the Lord Chancellor, and the judge between them had tied up the case most neatly, and Bertie found himself examined, not by the fearsome Ballantine, Mordaunt's counsel, but by the gentler Dr. Deane, counsel for Lady Mordaunt. Bertie was now a "witness" to throw light on Mordaunt's story, and all the questions were extraordinarily tame. Did he and the Princess give the Mordaunts wedding presents, take them to the theatre, and had

Sir Charles and the Prince acted as rival captains at a pigeon shoot at Hurlingham? What could have been more innocent? Then came the final, crucial question. "Has there ever been any improper familiarity or criminal act between yourself and Lady Mordaunt?"

How could any familiarity with the Prince of Wales be called "improper"—for that matter how could anything that he did with a lady be termed "criminal"? In manly accents, Bertie replied stoutly, "There has not." Loyal applause followed, duly suppressed by Lord Penzance. Ballantine rose, announced that he had "no further questions to ask his Royal Highness," and that was that. The judiciary had not exactly covered itself with glory, but the Queen's business had been done and Bertie rescued from a most unfortunate predicament.

But the whole case had clearly been a dreadful lesson for the Prince. It scarcely mattered if his denial in court was actually believed or not. As *Reynolds' Newspaper* asked with some asperity, why should a young married man pay weekly visits to a young married woman when her husband was away, if it was all so innocent? But that was not the point. Guilty or innocent, Bertie had been shown up, and everyone was ganging up on him. Gladstone, who dined with him after his court appearance and who had certainly been party to the hushing-up, wrote him a high-flown letter warning of dangers to the monarchy. Hawkers on Ludgate Hill were selling pamphlets bearing the Prince of Wales feathers and entitled *"Infidelities of a Prince"*—inside were reprints of parliamentary reports of the misadventures of the Prince Regent in 1820. Alexandra was obviously deeply hurt. She looked, one witness said, "lovely, but *very* sad," and left for Denmark on a lengthy visit to her parents.

For the first time in his life Bertie was actually booed in

public—once at the theatre, where he went with the Princess, and then again, two weeks later, when he was on his own at Ascot. On the first occasion he seemed shaken, but by the second he appeared to have recovered his panache, and in a gesture worthy of the "heavy swell," lit up a large cigar, waited to see a horse that he was interested in win a race, then smiled and raised his hat towards the watching crowd. This time they cheered, and Bertie was heard to mutter, "You seem to be in a better temper than you were this morning, damn you."

Bertie was always able to bounce back—in suitably rakish style—and on the surface, little was actually changed by the Mordaunt scandal. But he was no fool where his own interests were concerned, and must have seen the force of Gladstone's arguments—and even of the Queen's. Scandals like this were not just a confounded nuisance. They *were* a danger to the monarchy, and for the first time he was learning about the fickle nature of the public. He could no longer blissfully ignore it, behaving just as if his private life were no one's business but his own. There were two courses he could take—either give up his rake's life and conform to his mother's ideal of a moral monarchy, or else make absolutely sure that his private life stayed really private. There must be no more Mordaunt scandals to provide extra chapters for the author of *The Coming K— — —.*

Bertie had several months to ponder this, months when his popularity remained at lowest ebb and life seemed distinctly jaded. Victoria was pressing more than ever for him to give up those "unsuitable companions" of the last few years who had caused such trouble, and for a while it even seemed he might. The Duchess of Manchester seemed to be Victoria's particular bête noire—while she may not be doing anything "positively wrong" she had, Victoria insisted, done "more harm to society from her tone, her love of admiration and her 'fast' style than anyone."

Gladstone, more practical, tried dealing with what he considered the root of all of Bertie's troubles—his total lack of any proper occupation—and did his best to make the Queen agree to sending him to Ireland as her Viceroy. This was refused with queenly indignation and Bertie's morale and popularity continued to decline. Then when the "Prince of Wales problem" seemed to have become insoluble, his luck turned quite dramatically. Within a matter of a few weeks he was to have his popularity restored, his marriage revived, and to be given an incentive to put his rakish house in order.

Victorian plumbing lagged behind the other big advances that were being made in gracious living during the second half of the century. Drains were still dreadful, tainted water still brought widespread epidemics, and it was on a weekend with the Londesboroughs at Scarborough that Bertie and several of his party contracted typhoid from the stately drains. His friend Lord Chesterfield rapidly succumbed; so did a footman, and within a few days Bertie's condition was considered desperate.

This was in late November, 1871, ten years almost to the day since the Prince Consort succumbed to the identical disease. The coincidence turned what was anyhow a worrying occasion into a lesson on the mortality of princes and Bertie from a reprobate into the victim of cruel destiny. It was the sort of situation to bring out the sentimentality of the Victorians. For the Queen the stricken Prince was once again her "darling Bertie," and all the nation joined her in her bedside vigil. It was a long and anxious wait. Would Bertie follow Albert, if not to Heaven, at least to the Hereafter? The doctors offered little hope. In the immortal words of Alfred Austin,

> "Flash'd from his bed, the electric tidings came,
> He is not better, he is much the same."

And much the same he stayed right up until December 14, the exact anniversary of Albert's death. It was to be his day of crisis, and on that very evening Bertie's fever seemed to lift.

This was too much. Ignoble gossip and lurking republicanism were all swept aside in a great outburst of loyal relief. Slowly the Prince began to gather strength—suggesting incidentally that sex and overeating offered a better guard against disease than the earnestness and overwork indulged in by his father—and in the New Year, London was to witness the extraordinary spectacle of the Prince and the Princess driving to St. Paul's through cheering crowds to celebrate his recovery. Typhoid and luck had given him a chance to see that he never lost his popularity again.

The Bismarck
of Society

6

The Prince was playing billiards after dinner in the big billiard room at Marlborough House. It was the sort of evening he enjoyed. He had worked out the Marlborough House routine very much to suit himself. The food was rich and very good—so was the service. Bertie particularly objected to being kept waiting between courses, and even on formal evenings the men were not permitted to stay too long before they joined the ladies. One of his earliest innovations had been to bring in brandy and cigars in place of the traditional port and the nicotine-free evenings favored by Victoria. Then there would be whist and sometimes dancing for the guests.

But this particular evening was what he termed a "baccy," an informal all-male evening with just a few old friends and good cigars, champagne, high jinks, and billiards. He had originally started these affairs as something of a compensation for all the schoolboy jollity and comradeship that he had missed. Sometimes they ended up with cheerful gentlemen tobogganing down the stairs on tea trays or dueling with soda-water syphons. The princely sense of humor was notorious. He liked to see his friends around him happy, and almost anything was permitted as long as Bertie was amused as well. Royal informality could scarcely have gone further.

But there *were* limits—subtle, but nonetheless definite for that—and wise friends knew them and observed them by a sort of courtly instinct. But recently the Prince had grown slightly less predictable, and liberties could not be taken quite as freely now as in the past, particularly when he was out of sorts as he evidently was that night. His play was most erratic.* Finally, he missed a shot.

"Pull yourself together, Wales!" one of the jolly gentlemen exclaimed in what presumably he took to be the sort of manly humor Bertie relished. However, Bertie didn't. There was silence. Then the Prince beckoned an equerry and told him to fetch the gentleman's carriage. Thus the evening ended.

There were several incidents like this—for instance the evening at Sandringham when Sir Frederick Johnstone was acting strangely after dinner. Bertie, apparently concerned, said, "Freddy, Freddy, you're very drunk," at which the Baronet replied, "And Tum-tum you are *verrrry* fat," making fun not only of the Prince's girth, but also of his Coburg habit of a Germanic rolling of his R's. This was not well received. Bertie retired, and gave instructions that Sir Frederick would be leaving Sandringham *before* breakfast.

---

* Indeed, the Prince's eagerness at games generally exceeded his prowess at them. His bridge was unreliable, his shooting frequently erratic, and even at croquet his opponents would find it politic to let him win. His billiards playing was similar.

Such minor disagreeablenesses were soon made up. Bertie was too much the rake to be vindictive, and the horseplay would begin again when he was ready for it. But he was now approaching thirty. The first brave flush of freedom was behind him and as one looks at the photographs of him at this period—corpulent and bald, the pale eyes now beginning to protrude—a suspicion strikes one. Was he as happy as he should have been with so much to make life agreeable? Was it dyspepsia, or was he, could he possibly have been, a little bored? Did he enjoy his rakishness, or was it wearing just a little thin? According to Christopher Sykes, he retained "the child's pure enthusiasm" for his pleasures "which no amount of repetition" ever dimmed. But one wonders.

Certainly there seemed to be no falling off in the round of pleasures—or, as he still liked to call them, of his social duties —during the summer following his recovery from typhoid. Rather the reverse. That spring had found him back in Cannes and Paris, followed by a Mediterranean cruise with the Princess from which he returned to London at the beginning of June, fit and ready for the London season and even "stouter than before his illness." And however close his illness had brought him to Alexandra, it had done nothing to damp down his eagerness for other women. Early the next year, Francis Knollys, Bertie's secretary, approached the young Lord Rosebery asking if the Prince of Wales and his brother, the Duke of Edinburgh, could use the Rosebery house as a place where they could entertain their "actress friends." Rosebery, despite his friendship for the Prince, refused, but other friends, it seems, were more accommodating. Cockfighting, too, still figured among the Prince's amusements.

But the whole function of his rakishness was changing. Previously it had clearly been a simple enough reaction to the repressions of his youth, but now it was something different. It had become a way of life, a habit, compensating now for fresh frustrations, and an outlet for his energy—all that he really had to fill a very empty life.

True he was married, father of five children, with riches, friends, immense prestige beyond the dreams of any ordinary man. But Bertie was no ordinary man. He was the Royal Heir. This was his one authentic role in life, and just as his adolescence is the story of a boy deprived of almost all that could make life exciting, so his middle years reveal him still deprived—of the royal power that he was trained to wield. This was a source of gathering frustration. For although he had kicked so hard against his father's "system" and quite rejected his morality, Bertie had still inherited a great deal of the genuine Albertine earnestness, and there is something quietly pathetic in the way that he was always so eager to perform his "duties," almost to the point of mania. No one was more assiduous at keeping up the ceremonial niceties of his position. No one can have opened more public libraries, laid more foundation stones, graced more official ceremonies. A whole room was now put aside at Marlborough House to store his uniforms. Two valets were required to brush and care for them.

Still more did Bertie long for the substance of royal power. One of the great obsessions of his middle years was to be allowed a glimpse inside the red ministerial boxes which his mama still guarded so jealously at Windsor. That was too much to hope for but there were other things that he could do—attend the House of Lords, sit on committees for the housing of the poor, help to plan trade exhibitions. Nothing was too much trouble. Bertie was desperate to be of use. Even his friendships show him seeking power—Charles Dilke,

Joseph Chamberlain, and Randolph Churchill were all culti-
vated for their political advice—while abroad Bertie's eagerness to help solve the problems of world politics was a
perpetual source of worry to the Foreign Office, which never
knew when he might happen to meet the President of France
during those trips to Paris or Le Touquet.

The whole point was that Bertie had thoroughly ab-
sorbed the lessons Albert had taught him about royal power,
and now, ironically, it was Victoria, so anxious to perform
her "dearest Angel's" wish, who constantly frustrated him.
Why did she do this, when she might so easily have shared
much of the burden of her work with him, to their mutual
advantage? It is hard to know how much was jealousy, how
much the belief that it would be a disaster if the "poor
country" were entrusted to the Prince too soon. Certainly
she was piqued by the uprush of popularity for the Waleses
at the time of Bertie's recovery, and certainly she had the
feeling that her sacred mission was still unaccomplished. But
it was primarily thanks to her that the "unemployed youth"
Bagehot had described* was rapidly becoming an unemployed
middle-aged man. Gladstone was still trying to find him
some worthwhile occupation, but all attempts would founder
on Victoria's hostility. She loved her son when he was ill. She
stood by him when he was in trouble. She was quite recon-
ciled to his succeeding her—when the time came. But she was
adamant that in the meantime he was not "suitable" for any

---

* Walter Bagehot's celebrated study of *The English Constitution*
published in 1867 contained some pointed, not to say impertinent,
references to the Prince. As well as referring to Bertie as "an unemployed youth" and his mother as "an unmarried widow," he included
the warning that if the Prince finally reached the throne in middle or
old age, his idleness might well have turned him into little more than
"a pleasure-loving lounger, or an active, meddling fool."

genuine responsibility. He was too frivolous, and because of this the Queen effectively decreed that his frivolous life had to continue. And so it did, but with a difference.

It is a psychiatric commonplace to talk about the lust for power as a sublimation of the sex drive. In Bertie's case it is not being overfanciful to see the opposite, particularly in the middle seventies when Marlborough House was in its heyday. And gradually his rakishness and the pursuit of pleasure became the basis of a curious power structure of its own: increasingly it seemed as if he was ruling his own private pleasure kingdom in place of the nation as a whole. It was all rather odd, for his rule involved a strange mixture of high jinks and dignity, adultery and earnestness, pleasure and protocol. But it was all meticulously worked out. The rules were being carefully laid down. Frivolous he may have been, but Bertie possessed a very tidy mind and gradually he started to assert himself.

After his marriage the aristocracy had enthusiastically adopted the Waleses. Royalty was back within society and society had promptly made the most of it, and during those carefree years of the sixties Bertie had stood out as the epitome of smart society which had so largely made him what he was.

But all the time his social power was increasing. "Society" is by its very nature feudal and strictly deferential. Since Victoria stayed permanently immured at Windsor, it was inevitable that Marlborough House would rapidly become something of an alternative court, as Bertie and his bride began performing semi-royal functions which the Queen herself refused to do.

Now in the seventies something new was happening. Society originally created Bertie. Now the reverse was going on, and Bertie the rake was in command and changing society to suit himself.

There are innumerable examples of how he wielded his social power, but none more memorable than the short account by Mr. Christopher Sykes of how Bertie behaved towards Sykes's uncle and namesake, who was for many years the Prince's friend and courtier—the Victorian swell and courtier Christopher Sykes. Sykes, who was rich and handsome and no fool, had one fatal weakness. He was a passionate royal snob, and he was mesmerized by Bertie's presence. The Prince was his religion, and became his way of life. He venerated him, and Bertie's happiness became his main concern. This snobbery merely echoed, in extreme form, the emotion with which most of Bertie's followers regarded him; and as usual, Bertie exploited it unmercifully.

Sykes had a house in Yorkshire. This was useful. Sykes was a man of taste and never failed to provide exactly the food and company that Bertie liked. Each year, during St. Leger week at Doncaster races, he would entertain the Prince's party, with great opulence, at his house at Brankingham Thorpe. More useful still, he also had a house in Mayfair, and as a loyal courtier, Sykes suffered none of those strange scruples which had caused Rosebery to refuse the Prince the loan of his. Soon the anonymous Foreign Resident* would write of Sykes that "the social wishes of the Prince of Wales are his commands, and when the good Christopher receives an intimation from his royal master that he

* *Society in London,* which was published in 1885 under the pseudonym of "A foreign resident," is one of the best-informed sources of social gossip for the period, surveying as it does the Court, society, the stage, the literary scene, and high finance. The well-informed author was in fact not a foreigner, but T. H. S. Escott, the editor of the *Fortnightly Review.*

will dine with him on a certain evening and that he expects to meet certain guests, any previous engagement is cancelled and the banquet, big or small, is prepared forthwith. Mr. Sykes is, possibly by the mandate of royalty, unmarried."

Such loyalty, however onerous, was patently its own reward, but in poor Sykes's case it was to have a cruel twist. One evening, at the Marlborough Club, Bertie, "moved by heaven knows what joyous whim, emptied a glass of brandy over his friend's head." The great moment of Sykes's destiny had come. Unshaken and apparently unmoved, the perfect courtier replied, "As Your Royal Highness pleases." Loyalty, one would imagine, could have gone no further. But it did.

Sykes's reply made everybody laugh and Bertie, who loved a joke, soon realized that he had just invented a new party trick. From then on, no dinner party was complete without the wretched Sykes to act as the Prince's butt. He would pour brandy down his neck, assail him with soda water and champagne, dead gulls and live rabbits would be placed inside his bed, but Sykes would never lose his dignity, his temper, or his loyalty. Whatever Bertie did was sacred. Sykes would solemnly intone the words of loyal resignation—"as Your Royal Highness pleases"—and everyone would dutifully laugh.

Finally, of course, Sykes's obsession for the Prince virtually destroyed him. The money eventually ran out, the houses were both sold, and Sykes was left to linger on, slightly ridiculous by now, but still passionately loyal, a dreadful warning on the danger of the Prince's friendship.

The warning went unheeded, and Sykes's strange brand of self-destructive loyalty to Bertie seems to have been shared, in varying degrees, by the whole of smart society. Like Sykes it waited on the Prince's pleasure, and like him its only motto now was "As Your Royal Highness Pleases."

"Society in London," one commentator wrote, "in all it does, or abstains from doing, is . . . absolutely dependent on the initiative of royalty. It does precisely what royalty, or even those who are somewhat remotely connected with royalty, bids it to do."

Thanks to this strange infatuation, Bertie's power was absolute. The Foreign Resident called him "the Bismarck of Society," for he held supreme authority of social life and death. His most casual word against a person could mean social banishment: and equally his favor opened all the doors. He could reward those who pleased him with unsurpassable prestige—an invitation to a private dinner party, or to Marlborough House, or even, ultimate accolade, to Sandringham. Once this had happened, all else followed: one would be in demand and very fashionable and smart, touched with a little of the princely glamour as one of *his* special set. After this, life had little more to offer, save that the Prince should visit *you*. But if your house were large enough, if you could guarantee a really first-class table, decent shooting, preferably a racecourse nearby, cheerful conversation, and the sort of fun the Prince enjoyed, even this honor need not be ruled out. Much would depend upon the princely schedule. He was continually in demand, but he was still extremely energetic and loved new faces, loved to be amused.

It was well worth the effort to invite him. If he accepted, you could then send out invitations splendidly embossed—"To meet His Royal Highness, the Prince of Wales"—and for the dizzy days he spent with you, his standard would be fluttering above your battlements. He would undoubtedly be most charming—provided everything was to his taste. The gruff royal voice would praise your house, your furniture, your wife: he had a way of signifying what he liked and what he wanted. In return you naturally did everything you could to keep him happy. Before he came you would have planned the weekend like a military operation, and everything would circle round the princely tastes. There was much to take into account. You would have tried to hire one of his favorite chefs and have invited several of his current cronies who could be counted on to make him laugh. It was important too to arrange for good bridge players to keep him happy—no-nonsense players who would make sure the Prince would generally win. And you would also have found out as much as possible about his likes—*aubergines,* and ginger biscuits from Biarritz, and bath salts from Penthalicon's in Curzon Street. You would have ordered lobsters and champagne and ptarmigan and finally, as tactfully as possible, you would have inquired which of his mistresses it would be safest to invite. Such details make or break the pleasure of princes— and with Bertie the effort would be worth it.

With society so geared to Bertie's pleasure, it began mirroring *his* habits now. Almost by definition what he did or wore was fashionable. When he hurt his elbow and began shaking hands with his arm pressed tight against his side the idea caught on as the "Prince of Wales handshake." He introduced the homburg hat, the undone bottom waistcoat button, and the dinner jacket. Later in life he started playing lawn tennis to reduce his girth—and found that he had started yet another craze.

In fact his influence went much deeper than mere passing fashion. His whole style and attitude to life infected top society which, picking up its cue from him, eagerly adopted what it could. His style of conversation was distinctive. No wit himself, he mistrusted verbal cleverness and most enjoyed anecdotes—so these were carefully collected to amuse him. The Rothschilds even used to get their branch managers to cable good Jewish stories—which Bertie always loved—from the far reaches of the Austrian Empire. Intelligence, *per se,* was not considered quite the thing.

Instead there was that undemanding new invention—"general conversation," deferential, full of the sort of innuendo Bertie could understand. When the conversation failed there were other things to keep the great enemy, boredom, safely at bay. There was bridge, of course, and later, baccarat. And there was Bertie's speciality, the practical joke. There is no record of one of these ever played against the Prince, but this never stopped him from appreciating them when they were played on others. Rather the reverse. Nobody laughed louder when the shaving soap was put on the meringue, or when the live lobster was popped in Lord Dupplin's bed, or when the Duchess of Manchester made the butler drop the dinner service just behind the Duke. (When it transpired that the plates were cheap china and not Sèvres, he probably laughed louder still.)

But there was more to Bertie's influence upon society than slavish imitation of his slightest whim. It was subtler than that, and his extraordinary social power in the seventies seems to have drawn its strength from a profound community of interest between him and the portion of the aristocracy that he began to dominate. It was a period of decadence. The aristocracy, like Bertie, were falling back on social deference as their effective power declined. They were no longer leaders of the nation, patrons of taste and letters, as they had been even fifty years before. Compared with the group that glittered around the Prince Regent in his prime, Bertie's "smart set" appear distinctly seedy and provincial. But cornered as they were, between the plutocrats, the democrats and middle classes, they were still wealthy and still privileged enough to be grateful to Bertie for his leadership.

He was a rake and he could show them how to turn the pursuit of pleasure into a ritual, which would conquer their essential boredom as it had conquered his. He had been well trained and he was very much the creature of his age, with an unerring instinct for its luxury and comfort and its lack of taste. He really loved its huge meals, huge cigars, huge women, and huge ugly houses crammed with those great collections of appalling paintings. He had no doubts, no finer feelings to divert him. He wanted to enjoy himself and in the process he was quite prepared to discipline and lead his rakish little world on to its overfed inelegant doom.

But there was one important reservation in all this. Upsets like the Mordaunt scandal simply must not occur. Here he was in absolute agreement with Victoria. The only point where Bertie differed from his mother was on the remedy.

Her answer never varied: it was in essence still the solution worked out by Albert—a strictly moral and unsullied royal family to unite the nation. There must be no royal contact with corrupt society, which must be left to wither from its own excesses; and Bertie would have to toe the line, give up his rakish friends and entertainments, and live within his marriage vows.

For him this was clearly quite impossible. How could he possibly give up so much that made life bearable? During those happy years since his marriage, his life had become almost synonymous with society. He was at home within the aristocracy and felt one of them with all the passion of a convert. He was a rake who loved the rakish world he lived in.

But there *was* an answer to the problem. There was no need to change society—still less to change himself—provided everyone involved could see the danger of these public scandals, and appreciate that both the monarchy and the aristocracy had a shared interest in preventing them. Bertie was more cynical than his mother. All that was needed was discretion. Scandals would always happen if people set out to enjoy themselves, but society must keep them to itself. Even before the Mordaunt case he had written to Victoria about the "sad stories" he had been hearing, while in Paris, of high-life scandals going on in London. He said that he deplored them, but that he deplored "still more so the way in which (to use a common proverb) they 'wash their dirty linen in public.' " For Bertie, this was the real offense and one which the Mordaunt case surely brought home to one and all. Think of the wretched Mordaunt! He had attempted to revenge himself upon his wife and on his betters, but what had he achieved? Since the case he had become the most unpopular baronet in London, cold-shouldered at his club, cut in the House of Commons, and rightly treated as the pariah he was, and still married to his unfortunate wife. Thanks to the plea of her insanity the case could not go forward, and it was to take Sir Henry five more years before he was rid of her. That was what came of the upper classes trying to wash their dirty linen in public.

Examples such as this must have convinced most people round the Prince—if they were not convinced already—that discretion was the better part of class survival. Dog should not eat dog—nor baronet bite baronet.

For Bertie, this alone was not enough. Who knew what unforeseen disasters could occur with people in the grip of passion? If he and his friends were to continue with the life they loved, there would have to be unspoken rules of conduct

—and someone to enforce them should the need arise, some-one with power and prestige to act as social arbiter and counselor and judge. The role was there; who but the Prince could possibly fulfill it?

He was more than ready to oblige. Not for nothing was he Victoria's son and born to rule and lay down laws.

"His Royal Highness," wrote the Foreign Resident, "has developed into a sort of censor and inquisitor of society itself and of the court. As his royal mother is apt to sit in judgement on him, so he in turn criticises, counsels, castigates those who are subject to his authority. He is a prodigal of advice on matters great and small. Whether it be a conjugal quarrel or a questionable marriage, the pattern of a coat or the color of a frock, the Prince, if he is interested in those whom the matter concerns, volunteers his advice. . . . His Royal Highness wishes to be the mentor as well as the presiding genius of the aristocratic system in England."

And so, ironically, the unthinkable was happening, the poacher was turning gamekeeper, the most favored rake in England was setting himself up as moral censor and social arbiter.

Naturally this never cramped his own style—or restricted his rakishness. He could, and did, demand the full privileges going with his rank of "social despot." In effect he had a first-class season ticket to every famous house and bedroom that he wanted in the land. He never suffered from false modesty or sexual guilt: rather he looked upon each fresh affair as one more royal favor gracefully bestowed, and most women in his circle seem to have felt the same. His personal prestige was so exaggerated within society that his amours were generally regarded as something above the rules of

Young Bertie, a wistful child—an early portrait of the Prince of Wales by F. X. Winterhalter

William Gordon Davis

Mansell Collection

The well-dressed Prince, complete with beard to hide a weak chin
The New York Public Library, Branch Libraries, Picture Collection

THE ROYAL ROAD TO LEARNING.

How *Punch* saw the charmed arrival of the Prince at Oxford University, surrounded by obsequious academics. Bertie was the first royal heir to risk a university education since Henry V.

The royal groom, his bride, Alexandra, and his mother, Queen Victoria

Proud parents Alexandra and Bertie and their first-born, ill-fated
"Eddy," Prince Albert Victor, Duke of Clarence, in 1864

The Prince and Princess of Wales

Catherine Walters, called "Skittles," who had affairs with many of Edward's friends

Radio Times Hulton Picture Library

"The Jersey Lily"—Mrs. Edward Langtry, who brought something new to the old, traditional role of royal mistress

Victoria and Albert Museum

Sarah Bernhardt, who made
the most of the Prince's admiration

*Radio Times Hulton Picture
Library*

" 'Ullo, Wales!" La Goulue
—queen of the cancan and
Bertie's most exuberant foreign friend

*Radio Times Hulton Picture
Library*

"The rare, the rather awful visits of Albert Edward, Prince of Wales,
to Windsor Castle"—as seen by Max Beerbohm

Victoria and Albert Museum

TRANBY CROFT.

SEP. 11, 1890.

1. GEN. O. WILLIAMS.
2. LORD COVENTRY.
3. LYCETT GREEN.
4. BERKELEY LEVETT.
5. MRS LYCETT GREEN.
6. LORD A. SOMERSET.
7. REUBEN SASSOON.
8. LORD E. SOMERSET.
9. STANLEY WILSON.
10. TYRWHITT WILSON (EQUERRY)
11. ARTHUR WILSON.
12. CHRISTOPHER SYKES.
13. COUNT LUDSKEW.
14. MISS NAYLOR.
15. MRS. GEN. O. WILLIAMS.
16. MRS. A. WILSON.
17. LIEUT. COL. SIR C. GORDON CUMMING.
18. H.R.H.
19. COUNTESS COVENTRY.
20. LADY BROUGHAM.

The house party Bertie would rather have forgotten—Tranby Croft

Bertie's "Darling Daisy," Countess of Warwick, in full plumage as
Queen of Assyria

H.R.H.The Prince of Wales.

The urbane and aging Prince of Wales as seen by Sir William Nicholson

The New York Public Library, Branch Libraries, Picture Collection

The royal yacht *Britannia*

Radio Times Hulton Picture Library

The royal horse Persimmon, who won the Derby for Bertie in 1898

The butt of foreign cartoonists: *Le Rire* shows Edward with the Japanese Emperor — "European diplomacy has produced another Siamese twin."

Below, *L'Assiette au Beurre* in 1903 depicts the French attitude toward Edward and England

L'Impudique Albion

Bertie became an eager motorist in late middle age—here at High-cliffe Castle, in July 1899, aboard Mr. Montagu's twelve-horsepower Daimler

The last of the line—the Honorable Mrs. Keppel

King Edward VII and Queen Alexandra, circa 1902

ordinary morality or behavior. It was another case of "as Your Royal Highness pleases." He had extraordinary license. There were far more eager women than he could ever cope with, each of them all too anxious for the mystic and social kudos of becoming one more royal mistress. Rumor began to credit him—as rumor invariably does in the case of the lecherous great—with superhuman stamina and power, while for a husband it was more duty than dishonor to allow a wife the chance of royal pleasure.

The Prince took all this very much for granted, using—but not abusing—all his opportunities. He had no taste for young unmarried girls within society; inexperience never had appealed to him, nor had the trouble that could follow. But he did like variety and also, far more dangerous this, excitement. Even by his middle thirties he showed no sign of settling into a fixed routine or personal relationship. Nor was his energy or gusto flagging as he continued to consume his women with the same energy with which he consumed his mountainous meals. There was a basic diet of everyday encounters with discreetly chosen "actresses"—of the sort that his invaluable secretary, Francis Knollys, had been so anxious to arrange for him at Rosebery's house. Slightly more special —*à la carte* rather than the *plat du jour*—were the married women of his circle; he would usually visit them in afternoons at their own homes when their husbands were in their clubs and the servants in the basement. By an unwritten law, nobody asked questions if the Prince's hansom cab was seen waiting outside particular front doors in Mayfair or Belgravia. Finally, of course, there were the *pièces de résistance*—the current beauties and the ladies in full princely favor who could be properly enjoyed in the discreet availability of a weekend house party. Once more the resourceful Knollys would take pains to ensure that such and such a lady was invited and that no embarrassments occurred in allocating rooms.

This was the one condition—the avoidance at all cost of scandal and embarrassment for Bertie—and it was one that he could rigidly enforce. Since he controlled society, he could make the rules, insisting that the primary condition of membership lay in keeping up appearances. Once one agreed on that, almost anything was possible.

This was the basis of the one original achievement of Bertie's life—the gradual creation of an exclusive social-sexual game for top society to play. It was a game in which he made the rules, offered the prizes, acted as umpire, and played personally with undiminished vigor until late middle age.

The essence of the game lay in the way that he himself combined the leadership of smart society with his particular brand of undercover rakishness. He could dispense the social honors and establish the pecking order in the exclusive group around him; and inevitably he did this on his own somewhat basic terms. Rank was important—so was wealth. He was emphatically no social revolutionary; he loved his duchesses, his stately homes, the whole rich rigmarole of upper-class society. But his own rakish standards also counted. He wanted fun—amusement, pleasure, sexual freedom. He enjoyed racy talk, loud company, and a distinctly worldly and amoral ambience in which to flourish. But at the same time all of this had to be conducted with formality and great discretion, and accordingly the game developed its unspoken rules, mirroring Bertie's own mentality. Those who were privileged to play it lived by two separate standards. Inside their small protected group, Bertie's own easy rakishness prevailed. As the Foreign

Resident described it, "husbands and wives may all be a little mixed; but then, though there is fusion there is no confusion. They understand each other so well. They have tacitly agreed to enjoy themselves according to their own taste. *'Fay ce que voudras'* is their motto."

But for the benefit of the outside world, the players rigidly adhered to the conventions; for impropriety has never been maintained with such propriety as among these eager friends and followers of Bertie. Taking their cue as usual from the Prince, they were determined churchgoers, and attendance at the Sunday morning service was becoming an increasingly important part of the weekend ritual. Overdressed and over-fed, they choired their hymns from A. and M. and nodded through the sermon, firm in the knowledge that the Prince approved and lunch was on the way.

Similarly they took great pains to maintain appearances among the servants. This was, of course, an even emptier ritual than the churchgoing. None can have known better what was going on than all those fascinated nonplaying members of the household in the servants' hall who dressed the ladies, served the meals, made the beds, and brought the bath water. But once again the rules were carefully prescribed. Servants were not supposed to know who slept with whom— and provided the game was played according to the rules it was assumed they wouldn't.

It would have been considered the height of impropriety to place guests conducting a liaison in a double bedroom or even rooms with a connecting door, "because of what the servants might have thought." Instead great care would go into the allocation of bedrooms so that consenting parties would not have too far to walk. Names would be written out and placed in small brass holders on the bedroom doors —to avoid unnecessary muddle—and a corresponding card placed by the bell indicator in the butler's pantry. That was as much as the servants were supposed to know. Once dinner had been served, the beds turned down, and the sandwiches and Malvern water placed by each bed (in case of night starvation), the servants would retire. The proprieties had been observed and the delightful game could start in earnest.

The only time this double standard raised its true colors was if anything went wrong. A scandal, a suicide, or worst of all, the hint of a divorce, and all the players would immediately form ranks. This was another of the rules. The player was disqualified immediately. The game, for him at any rate, was over. From then on his former friends would judge him, not by their private rules, but by the standards of the world at large.

This was the ultimate deterrent and no one was stricter than the Prince against those who broke his rules. It rarely happened—he saw to that. But on one rare occasion when it did all hell (or nearly all of it) broke loose.

The Game
Goes Wrong

7

By the mid-seventies life had emphatically picked up again for Bertie. The Mordaunt scandal had been long forgotten and his supremacy within society seemed unassailable. The social game was flourishing: discretion ruled and his whole rakish, pleasant life pursued its energetic, bustling routine. Paris in the spring, early summer back in London, Cowes for the yachting, Homburg for a cure, Scotland in autumn for the shooting, and then back in Sandringham for Christmas. Now in his early thirties, he was in perfect health and prime of life, distinctly overweight but with his appetites and energy quite unimpaired. With all his earlier problems solved it was perhaps inevitable that his mind should turn—as it usually did when he had nothing else to do—to his role as future sovereign.

It was the same old question—how could he be of use—particularly now with Victoria in her middle fifties showing no sign of giving up the ghost, or a particle of power to her son? All that she permitted—and this because it was the one thing she could scarcely forbid—was that Bertie should perform some of the ceremonies that she refused to do herself. This appealed to him of course, and it was something he was good at. By now he had made himself a competent impromptu speaker and "the old peacock," as his nephew Kaiser William was to call him, loved all the protocol, the splendor, and the dressing up of every royal occasion. It was presumably some compensation for the reality of power that he had always lacked, but no one believed more passionately in all the trappings and the dignities of monarchy. Therefore he naturally delighted in the fuss the Russians made of him and Alexandra when they attended the wedding in St. Petersburg of his brother Alfred and the Emperor's daughter, the Grand Duchess Marie, in January 1874. He was naturally angry at Victoria's refusal to allow him to accept the rank of honorary colonel of a Russian regiment which the Tsar offered him, but the sheer splendor of the welcome tickled his vanity. This was grandeur on a scale that he had never seen before— the great parade in his honor in St. Petersburg, the royal palaces placed at his disposal in Moscow, the boar hunt in which eighty animals were slaughtered. This was the life for Bertie, and the mood continued on his return to England. In May the Tsar paid a state visit to England and Bertie put on a splendid banquet in his honor at Marlborough House, with Gladstone and Disraeli both there to meet him.

It was a fancy-dress affair—although as a concession the Prime Minister, Disraeli, was permitted to attend in full court uniform. Alexandra, superbly jeweled, appeared as the wife of a Venetian doge, but as usual it was her husband who was the center of attention. It was a good excuse to indulge his love of ostentation—although he was possibly tempting fate to go as Charles I. Certainly the mind boggles at the vision of that portly figure tricked out in maroon satin, gold-embroidered velvet, and "waving a mass of fair cavalier curls" from beneath a diamond-trimmed black felt hat as he danced exuberantly till dawn. Disraeli said the scene was "gorgeous, brilliant, fantastic," and before long, Bertie and Disraeli were busily discussing a further enterprise in much the same high-flown vein. Disraeli, like his predecessor, Gladstone, was concerned about the "problem" of the Prince and how to keep him out of trouble. During one moment of exasperation he was to say that his "young Prince Hal" was more worry than the Balkans. But, unlike Gladstone, Disraeli managed to persuade the Queen to let her son do something useful for a change, and it was thanks to him that he reluctantly agreed that he should make a full state visit to her Indian Empire on her behalf.

Disraeli even wormed a grant of £112,000 from a not wildly enthusiastic House of Commons for the trip (the Queen herself refused to pay a penny) and saw to it that the Government of India would add another £100,000. This wasn't quite enough by Bertie's standards—the Russian trip had left him with exalted notions of magnificence. But otherwise the whole idea appealed to him enormously. It was a chance for just the sort of jaunt he loved and he was soon planning it with schoolboy gusto.

After the Queen and Parliament, the one remaining hurdle was his wife, who, not unnaturally, assumed that she would go. This he managed to avoid—sadly but very firmly. The children needed her and India was no place for a woman in her state of health. Instead he would be taking some of his jollier cronies such as the Duke of Sutherland, Lord "Sporting Joe" Aylesford, Lord Carrington, and Lord Charles Beresford. Altogether there were to be eighteen members of his personal suite, along with a botanist called Mudd, three chefs, a stud groom, and the Duke of Sutherland's piper.

Victoria, as usual, disapproved—but not on account of the rejected Alexandra. Bertie should have more "eminent" men in his entourage. But Bertie wanted to enjoy himself, and although he had to drop his plans for taking several dozen Life Guards with him, he finally steamed off to India in October 1875 as if embarking on the stag party of the century. If Disraeli really thought that this was to way to keep young Bertie out of trouble, he should have known his future royal sovereign better.

In fact the visit started well enough. Bertie exuded charm and *bonhommie* and duly impressed everyone he met. In Poona he stuck pigs and hunted cheetah, in Ceylon blazed away at elephants, and on the borders of Nepal he killed six fully grown tigers in a day. This was the life that Bertie really loved. There were race meetings in his honor and elaborate receptions, fireworks, and polo, and at Calcutta on New Year's Day there was even a performance of his favorite farce, *My Awful Dad*. Then came disaster.

Was the Almighty once again intent on giving Bertie something of a lesson? If so, He chose His moment well. For there was Bertie camped on the Sardah River and being treated to the largest hunt of his entire career—over a thousand trained elephants and twelve thousand beaters assembled by the ruler of Nepal, all to enable the Prince to shoot his tigers. Each day would end with a hot bath and a splendid dinner party at which the Prince, in evening dress, dispensed the honors. On the twentieth of February a letter came which must have brought the worries of the world that he had left so far behind into the very jungles of Nepal. Scandal was on the warpath once again and for once Bertie wasn't there to deal with it. Sporting Joe's wife had written asking her husband for a divorce.

The seventh Earl of Aylesford was almost the epitome of the rich, rakish, horsy set that Bertie liked. Not overbright, or overfaithful to his wife, he had been described as "a famous man to hounds, one of those heavyweights who by sheer artistry and skill could ride light when galloping over the big shire fences."* He was a well-known drinker, whorer, practical joker. Hardly surprisingly his wife had not felt any great need to be faithful to him. Like all sound members of the Bertie set, both had been following the *fay ce que voudras* rule—without apparent friction. Lady Aylesford had even enjoyed Bertie's attentions for a while, but Sporting Joe had lived up to his name, and either from stupidity or loyalty or both had barely seemed to notice. Since then the lively Lady Aylesford had played the field—currently with the married son of the Duke of Marlborough, Lord Blandford. Blandford was another close friend of Bertie's, and no sooner had Lord Aylesford departed than he moved to Aylesford country for the winter, installed his hunters in a nearby stable, and settled down to the pleasures of the saddle and the bed.

Had Bertie been on hand to play the "social despot," the rules of his secret game would undoubtedly have been observed. The Prince would have known what was going on. Blandford and Edith Aylesford would both have received a genial warning against letting things get out of hand, and all in good time Blandford would have taken himself and his horses back to the bosom of his family. Certainly there would have been no question of permitting them to cause a first-class scandal by eloping.

And similarly with Aylesford himself, poor Joe was not behaving as cuckolds were supposed to in the Bertie circle.

* Anita Leslie, *The Marlborough House Set.*

Again, everything would have been all right back in England, where Bertie could have calmed things down by telling Blandford to be more discreet and Aylesford to console himself with someone else's wife. But here, on the Sardah River, things were different. Aylesford—unnatural man—was pining for his wife. The situation was getting out of hand, and there was not a great deal that the Prince could do about it. Even so he did his best. He gave Lord Aylesford what advice and sympathy he could, told him that Blandford was "the greatest blackguard alive," and finally dispatched him aboard an elephant for the nearest railhead, along with firm instructions to sort the muddle out before it got any worse. This done, the Prince returned to hunting elephants.

Unfortunately, things weren't quite that simple and back in London there was nobody with Bertie's discretion and authority to stop the scandal escalating. Sporting Joe was certainly the last man to do so. However good he was with horses, he had a rough way with an erring wife, and within hours of reaching London he was proclaiming his intention of divorcing her. He would cite Blandford, and for good measure he repeated Bertie's kindly meant but injudicious words about Lord Blandford's blackguardry. This was soon round the London clubs, and everyone involved was becoming most excited. Sporting Joe, like many stupid men who tumble to the fact that they have been made fools of, suddenly decided that his honor was at stake and wanted to challenge Blandford to a duel. Two of Bertie's saner friends —Lords Hartington and Hardwicke—managed to calm him down, and convinced him that dueling was not merely illegal now but ludicrous. But neither could shake Joe's obstinate intention to divorce his wife. This brought the final villain of the piece onto the scene—Lord Blandford's younger brother, the wild and distinctly dangerous Lord Randolph Churchill.

By now the whole situation was a mixture of hot tempers and cold feet. Poor Edith Aylesford had been got at by her regiment of sisters and made to realize how much she stood to lose if she eloped: and Randolph Churchill and the Marlboroughs had performed the same unromantic work on Blandford. The two lovers—as lovers in such situations often do—were speedily returning to their senses. But Sporting Joe would not. He still insisted on his honor—and his divorce—and at this point Lord Randolph cabled the Prince, requesting him to use all his influence to make him change his mind.

It is impossible to know quite why the Prince refused. Perhaps he felt that after his own previous interest in the lady it would have been tasteless on his part to interfere. Perhaps he resented the way Lord Randolph had worded his telegram. Or possibly the relaxing pleasures of Cairo—the heat, the nightly banquets at the Gezirah Palace, Offenbach at the opera—had left him in no mood to get involved with problems back in England. But just this once his social instincts had deserted him. Lord Randolph, always a great man for jumping to conclusions, rapidly decided that the Prince was in cahoots with Aylesford to ship the unwanted Lady Aylesford off onto Blandford at whatever cost. This would seem so unlikely as to be almost laughable, but Churchill was a convincing and excited man. He felt great loyalty towards his brother and in a fit of bold Churchillian recklessness decided on a course that no one else in England would have dared consider. He resolved to blackmail Bertie.

That he so much as considered this was something of a tribute to the Prince's reputation as a power in society. Clearly Lord Randolph thought that Bertie—and Bertie

97

alone—possessed sufficient influence to damp down the whole unfortunate affair. That he was able to consider it was due entirely to Lady Aylesford. She and her lover were by now completely cowed by their relatives—and mostly, one imagines, by the ferocious Randolph. They had abandoned all thought of eloping: all that they wanted now was peace and a chance to forget the whole unfortunate affair. Above all they wanted to avoid the scandal of the divorce—and it was to do this that Lady Aylesford had offered Randolph the means of putting pressure on the Prince.

At this point the whole affair starts to resemble the Mordaunt scandal. As with that earlier upset, it was the woman who had broken down under the weight of family pressure and the threat of social obloquy. And as with the Mordaunt scandal, the interest hinged upon "indiscreet" letters written to her several years earlier by the Prince. In this case Lady Aylesford had quite a packet of them which she decided (or was persuaded) to hand over to Lord Randolph with the farfetched idea that they could be used to force the Prince to force Lord Aylesford to give up the divorce.

It was all very hypothetical. Perhaps it could have been accomplished—but not by wild Lord Randolph in the state of billowing self-confidence he was exhibiting by now. He even told his friends that "he held the Crown of England in his pocket," and finally and unforgivably called on neglected Alexandra at Marlborough House to tell her about her husband's old affair with Edith Aylesford and warn her that unless the Prince agreed to stop Lord Aylesford seeking his divorce, he would be dragged in and the letters published. The resulting scandal, said Lord Randolph helpfully, would be so great as to prevent the Prince from ever becoming King.

Churchill's behavior was obviously stupid—as well as cruel —and Bertie's reaction was predictable. He was tired and already irritated by the whole affair. Now at the news that Churchill—whom he had previously regarded as a friend—was blackmailing him and dragging in the innocent Alexandra, he exploded. Gone was that polished social diplomat, gone the urbane apostle of discretion. Instead he was an outraged husband, spluttering with anger at the treatment of his wife.

The rules of the secret game had broken down, and passion, which Bertie tried so hard to keep in place, was on the rampage. Like the hero of a high-flown melodrama, Bertie decided there was one way and one way only for a gentleman in his situation to behave—pistols at dawn, a deserted beach in Northern France, and he would be waiting for Lord Randolph with his seconds. Lord Beresford was accordingly dispatched from Cairo to London, via Brindisi, with his Prince's challenge for Lord Randolph Churchill.

It would have been a memorable meeting. Both men were brave and both were obstinate. Bertie was probably the better shot—but also the wider target, and both were extremely angry. But Churchill realized at once that simply by making the suggestion, Bertie had blundered. Duels were illegal, and whatever the outcome of such an encounter, the monarchy would obviously suffer. The whole idea was so unthinkable that he felt justified in instantly replying to decline the challenge. At the same time he could not resist taunting Bertie with the insinuation that *he* had known the duel was impossible—and so was pretending to be braver than he was. This was unfair—as well as most insulting. Bertie was patently sincere about the challenge, and left to himself would certainly have followed the whole thing through.

Churchill's reply was brought back by Beresford to Malta in early April. One can imagine Bertie's feelings as he read it but, anger apart, there wasn't much that he could do. By his ill-judged but all too understandable behavior, he had completely lost control of the situation. The scandal would roll on, Aylesford would sue for his divorce, and Churchill would make sure that the Prince's letters were made public. Small matter whether the letters were deeply compromising or—as Bertie angrily maintained—merely quite innocent and friendly notes scribbled to an old acquaintance. After the Mordaunt scandal, that would be too much for the open-minded Englishman to swallow, and besides, Lady Aylesford had obviously told Lord Randolph much more about her past affairs and her relationship with Bertie. Who knew what further dirty linen would get washed in public once the divorce began? If this occurred—and with the reckless Randolph on the scene the odds were that it would—the repercussions could be frightful; more outcry from the outraged middle classes, more propaganda from republicans, an end to Bertie's social leadership and even, as Lord Randolph had warned Princess Alexandra, a threat to the Prince's ultimate succession to the throne.

It was a crisis, and Bertie knew that in crises he had one firm ally to fall back on—Queen Victoria. She had stood by him in the Mordaunt scandal, and he would have to count on her doing so again. It was no time for him to stand on his dignity and he could obviously have no further dealings personally with Churchill. So ten days after receiving the insulting answer to his challenge, he dispatched a message to his mother explaining what had happened, assuring her of his total innocence and begging for support. It was a little ignominious and touching for him to turn to her like this. The Queen lumbered to the rescue, cabling back her confidence to Bertie and using her influence at once to get a settlement. As in the Mordaunt case, the Queen was showing that her concern for the monarchy and the succession outweighed her disapproval of Bertie's rakishness and the disgraceful company he kept.

Disraeli had already done his best to calm matters down by trying to persuade Churchill to apologize to Bertie, and Aylesford to give up the divorce. Neither had yet agreed, but Victoria's influence now began to count. She made a great show of solidarity with Bertie, bolstering his confidence and telling him that there was no reason to stay away from Britain until the trouble had blown over. She also made her influence felt on Churchill and Blandford through her friendship with their parents, and indirectly started to work on Aylesford to make him change his mind.

Backed by this show of firm maternal confidence, Bertie summoned the boldest face he could and made a most resolute return to England, meeting Alexandra at sea off the Isle of Wight, being greeted by the rest of the family at Portsmouth, and then attending a gala performance in his honor at Covent Garden that same evening. Considering the rumors that were in the air, and remembering the way the crowd had booed him and the Princess after the Mordaunt scandal, this was courageous—and the Prince was duly rewarded for his courage. The crowds in the street cheered him and in the opera house he received a standing ovation from the audience. The very next day Lord Hardwicke came to Marlborough House with the news that Aylesford had decided that, in order to avoid great public scandal, he would call off the divorce. Sporting Joe had finally lived up to his name, and almost overnight Lord Randolph seemed to have become the most unpopular man in London.

Thanks to the Queen and to Disraeli, the Prince's near-catastrophe had been avoided. Thanks also to the sense of solidarity among the aristocrats involved against the maverick wildness of Churchill, the Prince's undisputed leadership of society could continue and the succession was freed from the threat of major scandal.

From the losers of the affair, society and the Court exacted discreet but nonetheless effective vengeance. Lord Randolph was persuaded by his family to sign a grudging note of apology to Bertie—despite which it was to be ten years before his former friend would finally consent to talk to him again. Lady Aylesford and Blandford lost their places in society, as they had feared they would, but went on with their association. Sporting Joe became increasingly drunken and pathetic, failing to obtain his divorce some five years later when he again attempted to rid himself of Edith, and ending up a hard-drinking rancher in the State of Texas. As for the Prince, his victory was complete. The Aylesford affair was the nearest he had come to losing his control upon society. He made sure he never did again.

The Rake Steps Out

8

One fine May evening in 1877 the Prince of Wales went to the opera. Alexandra was conveniently away, staying in far-off Athens with her brother, the King of Greece; and when the opera ended, Bertie drove on to Kensington for dinner with his friend Sir Allen Young, the Arctic explorer. Thanks to efficient staff-work by his secretary, Knollys, Bertie was seated next to the one young lady he had especially asked to meet—the twenty-three-year-old daughter of a clergyman. But neither the Prince's interest, nor the fact that all London was talking about her at the time, seemed to affect the lady's natural modesty.

She was distinctly overcome by the princely presence, and barely uttered more than the briefest of replies to Bertie's questions. Her husband, also present, has generally been described as "colorless" and seems to have lived up to his reputation. But none of this mattered. With her extraordinary eyes, Greek profile, and entrancing figure, the lady made the evening. Bertie was obviously delighted with her and he responded as he always did with pretty women, praising his host, charming the guests with gruff good humor, enjoying Sir Allen's excellent cuisine, and showing that he was "bent on making the evening a jolly one." Thanks to him it was—and before the Princess had returned from Athens, the clergyman's daughter was his mistress.

One wonders if the Prince knew quite what he was in for, for this shy woman with the dreary husband was unlike any other woman he had slept with. She was born Emily Charlotte le Breton but since her marriage to a sporting Belfast widower, she had been known as Mrs. Edward Langtry, "the Jersey Lily." She was a phenomenon, a symbol of a whole new style of womanhood, and just as her affair with Bertie capped her extraordinary career, so did it also bring a lasting change to Bertie's public image. More interesting still, it changed the whole course of his rake's progress.

In some ways she is difficult to account for. Lillie Langtry was a star. According to Richard Le Gallienne,* who knew her well, just as Tennyson symbolized poetry for the late Victorians, Gladstone politics, and Irving the theatre, so "the Lily" was almost instantly recognized as the personification of female beauty. Certainly her rise to fame seems to have been quite effortless and quite inevitable, and during her prime she enjoyed that special status of the star which disarms all (or almost all) criticism and places her above convention.

As usual with such living legends, there is little in her birth or background to explain all this. Her family was middle class and her father, who was Dean of Jersey, was as

---

* Richard le Gallienne (1866-1947) was a poet, essayist, and man about town whose book, *The Romance of the Nineties,* is an invaluable firsthand source on the leading characters of the period.

solemn and conventional as deans still were in those days. Her beauty was evidently inherited from her mother, who was described by Charles Kingsley while she was still a girl as "the most bewitchingly beautiful creature" he had ever seen. Her childhood was idyllic and her ability to cope with males started early. She was the only daughter among six brothers and as she said, "I was quick to perceive that, in order to take part in their sports and not to be left out in the cold, I must steady my nerves, control my tears, and look at things from a boy's point of view." She learned these lessons well. She was extremely tough, extremely practical, and while she could appear the acme of the wilting female she never ceased to be something of an Amazon.

At first she seemed little more than that well-known figure the beautiful young lady from the provinces with a romantic nature and a keen eye for the main chance. She spotted Langtry when he sailed to Jersey in his luxurious yacht, *Red Gauntlet,* married him despite the Dean's objections, and promptly sailed away with him for England, still wearing the traveling gown in which she wedded. After that short romantic honeymoon, Langtry was never to have her to himself again.

They reached London in January 1877 and almost at once the inevitable occurred. As a good Belfast man, widower Langtry knew nobody in London and the ill-assorted couple set out to see the sights. At the London Aquarium, of all places, they met Lord Ranelagh, whose daughters Lillie knew in Jersey. His Lordship asked them for the weekend to his house in Fulham. Lillie's career had started—Langtry's was almost over.

It was a stately progress. From Lord Ranelagh's at Fulham, the Langtrys were invited to Lady Sebright's for one of her at-homes, and from that first evening Lillie showed an unerring instinct for success. Perhaps it really was pure chance that made her choose a very simple square-cut dress and not to wear her jewels, and to have her hair "twisted carelessly on the nape of my neck in a knot."* She always claimed it was. As she explained years later in her memoirs, one of her brothers had just died and she was still in mourning. But when she goes on to tell what happened, one has the feeling that she overplays the artless innocent. "Very meekly I glided into the drawing room which was filled with a typical London crush, was presented to my hostess, and then retired to a chair in a remote corner, feeling very unsmart and countrified. Fancy my surprise when I became the center of attraction and, after a few months, I found that half the people in the room seemed bent on making my acquaintance."

Innocence or instinct or careful calculation—the result was all the same: the shyness marked her out from all the over-dressed and pushing social gorgons who surrounded her. The simplicity of dress underlined her beauty. Nor could anyone have found a better spot to launch a social debut than that particular drawing room on that particular night. For Whistler was there and so was Millais and so was Henry Irving, all of them professionally attuned to spot a new style of female beauty and each of them more than capable of publicizing it. Millais in fact immediately asked to paint her —and his portrait of her with a Jersey lily in her hand was to become the talking point of that year's Royal Academy. Whistler and Irving both tried to take her out to supper.

Lillie Langtry's name was made that night. It was as if London, without knowing it, had been anxiously awaiting her. Next morning the Langtrys found their hall table piled with invitations to lunch, to dance, to dine. At her first dinner party she met Lord Randolph Churchill, who wrote to

* Lillie Langtry, *The Days I Knew.*

tell his wife that he "took into dinner a Mrs. Langtry, a most beautiful creature, quite unknown, very poor, and they say has but one black dress."

She was not unknown for long. Within a few weeks, people at receptions were standing on chairs to see her. Lord Hartington was tearing lilies from his pool and throwing them, not only at her feet, but even over her coachman. A girl in a black gown sitting quietly in Hyde Park was mistaken for her and mobbed so badly by the crowd that she was taken to St. George's Hospital. Before long, Lillie's famous black dress was wearing out, and she appeared at a ball in a classically severe white velvet dress embroidered with pearls. The dancing stopped as she swept in through the doors.

There were several elements within this extraordinary *succès fou.* One was her actual type of beauty; this in itself was new and started a new fashion in female faces. With her thick hair and flawless features she had a melting soulfulness which contrasted with all the brassy harlots and the haughty *grandes dames* of the previous decade. Whale-boned, firm-jawed, sharp-featured, they were all hard girls. Lillie had gentle features and refused to lace her generous body: she was femininity in person. Another cause of her success was undoubtedly a subtle but important shift in popular morality. The tide was slightly turning against high Victorian censoriousness and a new, widespread cult of womanhood had started. The famous "New Woman" of the late nineteenth century was to take many forms—from Florence Nightingale and George Eliot to the heroines of Ouida's novels and the suffragettes. But one important early result of the movement was to make female sexiness acceptable provided it was gift-wrapped with sufficient sentiment. The "beauty" could now become a popular heroine—and thanks to photography she did. A few daring, photogenic society ladies had already gone public. Prim, coy, and sentimental, their features were becoming famous from the pale brown photographs which enterprising photographers were already putting on display and selling. The multitude was learning to lust after its social betters—Mrs. Cornwallis-West of the golden hair and well-cut riding kit, Mrs. Luke Wheeler with the come-hither eyes, and the Junoesque Duchess of Leinster almost bursting from her ball dress. All of these women were already in society and graciously accepting the publicity from vanity or for the social kudos. Lillie was different. She was the first outsider to use publicity to take society by storm.

How well, and it seems how effortlessly, she did it! How avidly her audience pursued her! She had the true self-publicist's flair for instant self-projection and knew exactly how to use a trade-mark to create a talking point—the modesty, the way she did her hair, the famous little black dress that caught Lord Randolph's fancy. Then came Millais's lily and the different features other women copied when she became the height of fashion—"the Langtry knot" in which she wore her hair, the famous "Langtry hats" which even Alexandra wore, the "Langtry shoes" which soon sold in their thousands.

Publicity alone was not its own reward, but what it did for her was to offer her a status which was quite unique. She was not a tart, nor a commonplace loose woman, nor a courtesan in the style of the famous *grandes horizontales* of the French *Belle Epoque.* She kept her independence and her dignity and slept her way invulnerably and calmly up through society in six short if energetic months. An extraordinary achievement! She and the sadly treated Mr. Langtry took a small house in Mayfair for the season. One of her earliest lovers was Morton Frewen, a good-looking

young adventurer and horseman.* Her opening gambit was
to stare at him with large blue eyes and ask, "What are your
spiritual beliefs?" Suitably impressed, the handsome Frewen
was soon in hot pursuit. He was as soon rewarded. In return
he was permitted to present her with a splendid chestnut
hack, teach her to ride it, and be seen with her in Rotten
Row. By then he had evidently served his turn. She wanted
something more than penniless, good-looking lovers, and as
her fame spread there was no problem getting what she
wanted.

During those crowded weeks before she met the Prince
she seems to have become a sort of amorous Clapham Junc-
tion. There was Lord Lonsdale and Sir George Chetwyn and
Prince Rudolph of Austria and the King of the Belgians
(who used to call on her at nine in the morning). It was
never very clear which of them were lovers and which of
them mere admirers. Not that it mattered very much, except
to Mr. Langtry, who was becoming understandably put out
by what was going on. Incredibly, Lillie seems to have kept
the truth of her affairs from him, but there are worse things
than unfaithfulness for an aging husband to put up with
from a young ambitious wife. As she wrote blandly in her
memoirs, "My husband greatly disliked all the publicity,
sometimes losing his temper and blaming *me!* As can be
readily understood, his position was an onerous one, for,
aside from his vexation at seeing his wife stared at as a
species of phenomenon, we never went out but that he was
kept busy hurrying me from one place to another as he saw
the familiar crowds beginning to assemble."

* Not long after his Langtry episode, Frewen departed for America,
where he finally married one of the Jerome sisters, thus becoming
brother-in-law to Randolph Churchill and Winston Churchill's uncle.

This passage probably explains something of how she was able to achieve the freedom that she did. Poor henpecked Langtry, scurrying from drawing room to drawing room in the exhausting shadow of his celebrated wife, must have been grateful for an hour or two off duty when she was riding in the Row or doing whatever else she did with one or other of her titled followers. She was even able to find time to go sailing for a few days with Bertie's younger brother Leopold, off the Isle of Wight, hiding below decks until they were safely out of sight of the telescope at Osborne House.*

In this whirlwind rise to fame she was much more than just a mistress—she was a national celebrity, a public figure. Sleeping with her, however pleasant, was really secondary to being seen with her. Thanks to publicity, thanks to the spirit of the times, she became accepted as a fashion when she met Bertie. She had made her own exclusive set of rules, and just as the graph of her success had to converge on Bertie, so he in turn could be openly accepted as merely one more social figure paying his respects to fashion.

This explains what is otherwise quite inexplicable—the fact that Bertie, who until now had always been the most discreet of rakes, was suddenly being seen in public with her, regularly riding in the Park, watched by an admiring crowd, dining with her several times a week, and constantly meeting her at weekend parties. Her less distinguished lovers now kept their distance. "Quite impossible to compete with Prince Rudolph, much less the Prince of Wales," wrote Morton Frewen, although he added philosophically that he "had the joy of seeing her riding my horse when out exercising

* This didn't stop Victoria from having her suspicions. When Leopold was ill, Victoria visited his bedroom, recognized a portrait of la Langtry above his bed—and promptly removed it.

with H.R.H. Anyway lilies can be dreadfully boring when not planted in a bed!"

This riding together soon became a daily routine for Lillie and the Prince, and everybody knew. On one occasion in the evening Bertie detained her until nine o'clock, although she was expected at a Belgravia dinner party at eight-thirty. She rushed home to a grumbling husband, hurriedly changed her dress, and reached Belgravia more than an hour late. There was no need to have worried. Her hostess, although a *grande dame* of the old school, had already heard that she was riding with the Prince: dinner was automatically waited until her arrival.

It was a revealing incident for it shows the way in which she was becoming something completely new in Bertie's life —an acknowledged royal mistress; but one must emphasize the fact that she remained a fashionable celebrity on her own terms. This was important, for it meant that, unlike all Bertie's previous mistresses, she could be admired and entertained for her own sake. Fashionable curiosity about her knew no bounds—finally Victoria herself succumbed, and Mrs. Langtry was commanded to appear at one of Her Majesty's afternoon drawing rooms. Normally the Queen retired early from the scene, and Lillie was due to be presented late in the afternoon when the Princess of Wales had taken over. But on this occasion Victoria was obviously determined to see her famous subject, and stayed grimly on until Lillie, in ivory brocade and trailing yellow roses, was called to make her curtsy. "Queen Victoria," she wrote later, "looked straight in front of her and extended her hand in rather a perfunctory manner." After the Queen's reactions to her son's previous mistresses, it is surprising that this is all she did.

But if Victoria's curiosity was glacial, others were more accommodating, and perhaps the most startling convert to her charms was Gladstone, who, by now Prime Minister once again, called at the house in Mayfair, gave her improving books to read, and was so taken with her that he made no objection when she made social capital out of his visits. He even gave her the rare privilege of his private code sign, which guaranteed that any letters that she wrote him would not be opened by his secretaries. Gladstone, like everybody else, was half in love with her and fascinated by this living legend.

For Victoria and Gladstone both to have accepted the acknowledged mistress of the Prince of Wales was an extraordinary event—which could have happened only if both had been quite certain that she represented no danger to the throne. This was Lillie's great achievement. She could be who she was without a threat of scandal to the Prince. Some of the credit for all this should certainly have gone to "colorless" Edward Langtry—one of the unsung heroes of Victorian England if ever there was one. He was the perfect cuckold, and his somewhat seedy presence guaranteed that there would be no risk of a divorce. He was so much of a nonentity, removed from his Belfast element, that he could be browbeaten by his wife and totally overawed by the grand world she moved in. No one appears to have been grateful to him—or even to have felt sorry for him. When he began "grumbling," Lillie would usually send him off fishing, which he enjoyed far more than smart society. Only once is it recorded that this most accommodating of human worms actually turned—this when the Langtrys were both staying for a weekend with Lord Malmesbury. Lillie had been writing at the desk. Langtry held up the blotter to the mirror, and saw that she had been writing a love letter to the Prince of Wales. There was a scene. Langtry was furious, Lillie in tears, but in the end the only upshot of it all was that Malmesbury gave

orders to his servants that in future his guests' blotting paper
was to be changed regularly each day.

The true beneficiary of Lillie's rise to fame was, of course,
Bertie, whose love life was abruptly changing—for the better.
Not only was the lady beautiful and more than willing—
most of the women were whom Bertie cast his eye on. But
she was actually acceptable to everyone—to Gladstone, to
Victoria, to society, and to the ordinary people in the Park.
Even Alexandra seems to have accepted her—and Bertie
liked his wife to like his mistresses. All this was so different
from his previous amours, with their fears of scandal and
anxieties about compromising letters.

With fashionable Lillie there was none of this. Times
were changing—so were people's attitudes—and it was soon
quite obvious that Lillie, far from threatening the Prince's
reputation, was actually enhancing it. Perhaps Victoria and
the "Higher Classes" had always overestimated the extent of
public prudery. Or possibly the fickleness of popular opinion
was even greater then than now. But people were clearly not
averse now to the idea of a stylish Prince of Wales who
dressed well, enjoyed life, and had a sharp eye for a pretty
woman. Bertie the Rake was finally achieving public recog-
nition.

Bertie's affair with Lillie Langtry lasted just over five years.
He was delighted with her and extremely happy—and as
usual when he was happy he was more thoughtful to Alexandra. In 1879 he even renounced his customary trip *en
garçon* to Homburg and took the Princess instead to visit her
family in Copenhagen. But the position of mistress to the
Prince of Wales was always precarious—even for as powerful
a personality as Lillie. Fashion—and Bertie's affections—
were changeable, and her position could not last forever.
He never had made any great pretense of being faithful to

her—that would have been *too* much to expect—and finally in 1881 the crisis came. She was no longer quite the fashionable figure she had been. Money was getting short, "Mr. Langtry," as she put it, "fished perpetually," and his estates in Ireland were in a bad way. The bailiffs moved into the little house in Mayfair, and then to add to the confusion, Lillie produced a daughter. According to one story, when this happened, Bertie flipped a coin to decide if he could be the father; the story does not relate what it decided.

But parenthood had never been the aim of Bertie's love affairs, and the appearance of a little Langtry seems to have spelled the end of the romance. He was quite heartless in these matters, and besides, Lillie was now becoming what she had never been before—vulnerable to gossip and a potential source of scandal. There were disturbing rumors of divorce and Bertie suddenly had other interests. Society behaved to her as society always does, and hostesses who sought the friendship of the Prince's mistress now turned their backs on the discarded woman. There was not even Mr. Gladstone's unworldly interest to console her.

Not that she wanted consolation. Now came Lillie Langtry's most impressive moment. Instead of quietly subsiding in the prescribed style with her grief and shame, she came bouncing back, first in a charity performance of *She Stoops to Conquer,* where her brazen presence drew what the *Times* described as "the most distinguished audience ever seen in a theatre," and then to a career as a professional actress. Bertie is generally praised for the way he now helped her, by persuading Sir Squire Bancroft of the Haymarket Theatre to give her her chance, but it would seem to have been the least that he could do, and anyhow Bancroft was not exactly risking his theatre on some shy unknown. Certainly the Prince did everything he could to help her new career, coming up specially from Sandringham to see the play and to attend a glittering midnight supper with her in his honor. And afterwards the glamour of the Prince's name ensured her great success in America, where she lived lavishly, earned enormously, and finally amassed enough to return to England, put on weight, breed racehorses, and marry herself a baronet after Langtry's death. One feels that she deserved it.

The Rake at Forty

9

The Prince was forty when his affair with Lillie Langtry ended, and for the first time since his marriage it is hard not to feel a little sorry for him—at any rate as sorry as one can for somebody with £120,000 a year, three splendid houses, an understanding wife, a yacht, five children, and all the sex and society he desires at his command.

Spoiled youths are often irritating, but spoiled middle-aged men are rather sad: with Bertie the pursuit of pleasure had been so successful that it was now becoming something of a trap. Belly and baccarat, bridge and bed—the same routine, the same old round, had been going on for twenty years, and now that the novelty of Lillie Langtry had worn off there seemed a certain flavor of futility to it all. The spontaneity and the excitement of the early years had gone, but pleasure was still his main concern in life—for want of any other. It was a habit now, a way of vigorously marking time until through death or—most unlikely this—through abdication, Victoria admitted him at last to his inheritance.

The flesh gave no sign of failing him. He was as eager now as he had been at twenty-two, as steadily promiscuous, as blithely self-indulgent. He was still ready for the day's fresh amorous adventure, still bustling through the social round, still overeating, gambling, weekending, traveling abroad *en garçon,* and enjoying his priapic great cigars.

Where the dissatisfaction showed was not in a slackening of pleasure, but in his profound anxiety to be of use. Instead of quietly subsiding with the years, this had grown steadily more acute and was now becoming something of a chronic malady. Unfortunately his pleasure-seeking had persuaded everyone—especially the Queen—that he was still as frivolous as ever, an overweight and bearded social butterfly who lacked the solemn qualities needed for serious Victorian affairs.

This caused him genuine distress, for underneath the socializing, womanizing, and incessant busybodying lay a frustrated man of action. He was extremely brave and energetic and persistent, as he showed during his drive through disaffected Cork in April 1885 when he continued, angry but quite unbowed, through a hail of catcalls, jeers, and rotten vegetables. But opportunities like this were rare, and three years earlier he had been deeply disappointed when Victoria refused to let him join the British expedition to Egypt which defeated Arabi Pasha at the battle of Tel-el-Kebir. This refusal of the Queen's was particularly galling, if only because so many of his friends were there, enjoying the excitement and sharing the glory. The wild Lord Charles Beresford had personally commanded the gunboat *Condor,* which had bombarded Alexandria and earned him a hero's welcome on his return to England. Even Bertie's brother Connaught had been given command of a Guards Brigade which marched on Cairo from Port Said. Whereas he, a full Field Marshal now, still had experienced no active service, and had to endure cartoons in the foreign press which showed him as a playboy soldier, with epaulettes and decorations fighting the battle of the flowers at Cannes.

More serious for Bertie, the Queen still indignantly refused to let him read government papers passing between Ministers and herself. Gladstone had loyally attempted to persuade the Queen to change her mind, to no avail. Victoria was quite determined to keep her son and heir from meddling in affairs of state until his time came—and she was no longer there to witness the result. The matriarchal veto was still in force, the vicious circle still unbroken: the Prince was left unemployed and so continued with his round of pleasures—and because of his pleasures he was considered unsuitable to be employed.

It was unfair and from his point of view unreasonable, but one suspects that Victoria was probably right. It is hard to take his political judgment too seriously. His socializing and the rake's life he had led left him no time for a sustained concern with politics. He was extremely *interested,* of course, and from time to time would show that he was passionately involved—as in his pro-French feelings and his dislike of Prussia, or in his sudden sympathy when confronted with the East End poor, such as the time when the liberal Lord Carrington took him to see the slums of Clerkenwell in 1884. But those confounded social duties *would* keep cropping up and distracting his attention. Even his great attempt to lend his prestige to solving the problem of the slums by joining a Royal Commission on the Housing of the Working Classes ultimately failed through this. He conscientiously attended several meetings, along with Lord Salisbury, Cardinal Manning, Sir Charles Dilke, and Lord Carrington. He spoke in the House of Lords and demanded urgent action from the government. Then, in March 1884, his brother the Duke of Albany expired in Cannes. Bertie was required to see the body home to England. For the two months following the funeral, Bertie felt obliged to stay abroad to avoid the tedium of strict court mourning. He was apologetic about "losing the thread of the inquiry," but it could not be helped, and although he attended the autumn meetings of the Commission, he never made the real contribution to the condition of the poor that he had once intended.

This was very much the story of his life. He was essentially a kindly, sentimental man, and on an emotional issue his heart could usually be counted on being firmly in the right place. But twenty years of flattery and pleasure had quite unfitted him for serious or consistent policy. Easily diverted and easily swayed, he was an impassioned dabbler who always overestimated the importance of the private contacts he enjoyed with royal relatives and friendly statesmen throughout Europe. True, he knew them all and had talked endlessly to them over a succession of rich dinners, grand state functions, hunting parties, and receptions—Gambetta and Bismarck, the Tsar and his dreadful nephew, the future Kaiser William, the Emperor of Austria and the King of Portugal. But when he tried to use these contacts to make his own sage contribution to diplomacy, the result was usually disastrous. Bismarck ran rings round him, the Kaiser snubbed him, the French loved him but made fun of him, and a succession of British foreign secretaries found they had to cope with his indiscretions and enthusiasms.

The Prince's friend Sir Charles Dilke put his finger on the trouble when he described how this most sociable of beings was always "a good deal under the influence of the last person who talks to him, so that he would sometimes reflect the Queen and sometimes reflect me, or Chamberlain, or some other Liberal who had been shaking his head at him." Dilke thought the Queen had more real brain power than her son and far more obstinacy, but despite this, "it is worth while talking seriously to the Prince. One seems to make no impression at the time . . . but he does listen all the same, and afterwards, when he is talking to someone else, brings out everything that you have said."

But at the same time the rakish life that he had so conscientiously pursued had inevitably helped to form his true political beliefs and prejudices. His real interests lay with the extremely rich and privileged, the landowners and plutocrats who formed the society he enjoyed and owned the big houses and estates he loved. Victoria might feel that the future of the country lay with the moral middle classes. Bertie at heart could not agree.

He was, as Dilke again remarked, "in fact a strong Conservative, and still stronger Jingo," abroad rumbustiously aggressive, at home a profound believer in the *status quo*. The only real exceptions that he made to this were when his pleasures prompted him, for when it suited him no one could appear more radical or democratic. His charm had grown with the years, and by his forties was formidable. He could get on with almost anyone. He, more than any other member of the Royal Family, possessed the common touch. He might be—and in fact frequently was—selfish, wrong-headed, arrogant, and mean, but nobody who met him ever seems to have disliked him. In any social situation he could invariably get his way, and he was always willing to employ this power and his immense prestige when it suited him.

From the beginning of his role as "social despot," he had always been quite willing to bend the rules of high society for anyone who pleased him. This did not "democratize"

English high society, which remained as snobbish and exclusive and probably as stupid as it had ever been. But it did bring a leavening of some unlikely outsiders who certainly helped lighten the social scene around the Prince. In his own private life he was the least exclusive of men and automatically assumed the right to open the doors of Marlborough House—and hence of polite society—to anyone he chose who happened to amuse or interest him or simply catch his eye. Various "adventuresses"—those scarlet women of the higher echelons of late Victorian harlotry—owed their entry and positions in society entirely to the Prince's backing. So did a number of ambitious and energetic American heiresses who would otherwise have been shunned by smart society as quite beyond the pale.

A few years earlier, Bertie had been involved with the glamourous Jennie Jerome, and then with her two effervescent sisters. Thanks entirely to the Prince's interest, smart society admitted them to its ranks. As Clara Jerome wrote, just a shade naïvely, "I don't know why, but people always seem to ask us whenever H.R.H. goes to them," and as usual, Bertie's interest in American heiresses started a fashion. Soon it was quite the thing for members of the British aristocracy to find their wives—and hopefully their financial salvation, too—among the daughters of the businessmen and bankers of America. It was a fashion which continued nearly half a century, and the most notable example was between Jennie Jerome and Lord Randolph Churchill.

Bertie's own predilections opened society in other ways. He was as vulnerable to the allure of wealth as to that of a pretty face—in some ways more so—especially as throughout his forty years as Prince of Wales he was perpetually short of money. Neither the Queen nor Parliament was sympathetically inclined to give additional finance for what was seen as

Bertie's extravagant and generally disreputable way of life—his gambling debts, his mistresses, his racing, and his perpetual holidays abroad.

In fact his rakish pleasures had never consumed more than a small proportion of his income. With the years he had grown quite stingy with his mistresses. He would be helpful to them—as he had been with Lillie Langtry—and usually extremely sympathetic, but there were no expensive jewels, no princely pensions when the affairs were over. Nor could his gaming debts be called enormous. The largest sum which changed hands in an evening's whist in 1865—this at a time when the Queen was worrying about Bertie's card debts—was £138, and two years later there had been nightly losses of £300 and £400 at White's. But losses like these were exceptional and since then his gambling debts had been kept "within reasonable bound," while the Prince claimed that his bets on horses often actually yielded him a small profit.

Most of his money was spent running his three establishments—Marlborough House, Sandringham, and Abergeldie, the Highland shooting lodge which he had bought in 1867. His parliamentary grant had risen now to £120,000 a year, but all the capital inherited from thrifty Albert had long been spent. He had a large staff to support and his official duties all cost money. More to the point, one must remember that he was living a rich man's life among the richest men in England—close friends like Hartington or Sutherland could have bought him out many times over. Bertie had learned the knack of thoroughly exploiting his wealthier friends—Savile and Richmond for the racing, Sykes for his London house and Hartington for regular weekends, Sutherland for shooting—but this was an extravagant world. Consumption was most conspicuous, luxury the order of the day, and it says much for the skill of his financial comptroller that his expenditure by the eighties was exceeding income by no more than an annual £20,000. This mounted up; by 1889 the Prince was reported to be so hard up that his hotels in Cannes and Homburg were besieged by financial touts and he was being pestered by moneylenders. The British ambassador in Paris even felt obliged to seek the assistance of the French police to head them off.

Bertie's close friendships with many of the leading Jewish families of his day, particularly the Rothschilds and Sassoons, can be and have been variously interpreted. They certainly did show his freedom from all form of social and religious prejudice. They also proved that when it suited him he was determined to dispense with the exclusive snobberies that ruled society. But it would be paying him too great a compliment to pretend that he was motivated primarily by such laudable intentions.

In fact, as with almost everything he did, his Jewish friendships stemmed in the first place from his love of pleasure: had he not been the rake he was, it is unlikely that the Rothschilds would have reached the House of Lords—or the Sassoons have penetrated the exclusive reaches of the Royal Enclosure. His feeling for these immensely wealthy social outsiders was profound and went back to his earliest manhood. As an undergraduate at Cambridge he had been impressed by the young Nathaniel de Rothschild, whose elegance and urbanity and seemingly limitless resources distinguished him from all the other wild young men of Trinity. Bertie was dazzled by him then—and he continued to be dazzled by the Rothschilds for the remainder of his life. There were times when Bertie "seemed almost to have a positive preference for Jewish society," and his friend the down-to-earth Lady Paget

wrote of the affinity which the Prince felt for the Rothschilds
and Sassoons. "He has the same luxurious tastes as the
Semites, the same love of pleasure and comfort."

This was quite evident. He felt particularly at home with
Rothschild hospitality, whether at Alfie Rothschild's appalling house at Tring or Ferdie Rothschild's great French
baronial pile at Waddesdon, or at one of the town houses of
"Rothschild Row" in Piccadilly or at the establishment of
Baron and Baroness Alphonse de Rothschild in Paris. Even
at Homburg there was a member of this omnipresent clan to
offer him hospitality—Baroness Willie Rothschild, whose
estate at Koenigstein Bertie would never fail to visit every
summer.

There was a lavishness, a full-blown and unashamed vul-
garity about the Rothschild houses that found an answering
chord in Bertie. Even today they strike one as his natural
habitat, and when he was entertained there his hosts tried so
much harder, spent so much more to make the Prince feel
wanted than Hartington or Savile or the Duke of Sutherland.
At No. 2 Piccadilly Alfie Rothschild would offer Melba and
Rubinstein and Liszt. At No. 3, when Ferdie arranged a ball
in honor of the Prince's friend the Crown Prince Rudolph of
Austria, he offered all the ladies on the guest list a dress each
from Doucet in Paris—something again that no English
aristocrat would dream of doing—even if he did query Lillie
Langtry when typically she ordered a petticoat as well.

The Prince's intimacy with the Sassoons and Rothschilds
was profound. He liked their food, their sense of humor,
and their cosmopolitanism. He used their international contacts and followed their advice. But underneath these qualities there was something else for which he valued them,
something that marked them out from all the other members
of society—their money.

For Bertie possessed the true rake's attitude to wealth. He was a great materialist and would have agreed with Byron when he wrote—"Money is power and pleasure and I like it vastly." Unlike Byron, he also liked people who possessed it, frankly regarding great wealth as proof positive of social worth. Money was power, and Bertie would always relish the company of those fortunate enough to exercise it.

How much the Prince's millionaire friends helped him with his own finances has always been something of a mystery. This was an age when "gentlemen never talked about money," but certainly Sir Ernest Cassel, another eminent Jewish banker and friend of Bertie's, helped him with his investments—and in return reaped the supreme reward of having the Prince as his guest at Biarritz each summer. Baron Maurice de Hirsch, an even wealthier outsider, whose social ambitions had been trodden on by continental royalty, found himself taken up by Bertie on a similar basis. Instead of Biarritz, he used to entertain the Prince at enormous shooting parties on his estate in Hungary—and when in England had the satisfaction of being invited to Marlborough House and Sandringham.

Plainly such men—as well as the Rothschilds and Sassoons—would find it easy to suggest worthwhile investments for the Prince—and to make sure that he would never come a cropper. Thanks to the help of friends like these, the princely finances steadily improved throughout the nineties, but it would be wrong to see his friendships with so many big financiers due entirely to what he could get out of them.

The Prince had a romantic attitude toward plutocrats. They represented action and excitement of the sort he loved. Brash, worldly, self-made men like Thomas Lipton, the grocery magnate, or Sir Blundell Maple, the furniture millionaire, were characters after his own distinctly worldly heart.

His rakish character could not appreciate too scrupulous an attitude in others and it was natural for him to have warmed to an opportunist visionary like Cecil Rhodes* from almost the beginning of his career.

Bertie's consuming interests, however, lay not with the politicians or the bold men of affairs, but with his social life, his love affairs, his dinners, and his trips abroad.

When his association with Lillie Langtry ended, there was no obvious public successor, if only because none of the Prince's other mistresses possessed sufficient public flair and personality to take her place. For a while at least he seemed content to return to his earlier practice of amorous discretion.

The nearest thing to a public liaison was with that supreme self-publicist, Sarah Bernhardt. One must presume that the Prince became the lover of this living legend. (She was, in fact, surprisingly reticent upon the subject when she came to write her memoirs.) Most men did who wanted to and were in a position to help her career, and from her first appearance on the London stage in 1879 she shrewdly realized that the Prince's support was necessary if she were to take the town by storm. As luck would have it he had just left for Paris when she arrived, and the princely red carpet was still on the platform at Charing Cross as if to welcome her. But though it was not Bertie, but his brother the Duke of Connaught who was in the royal box on her opening night at the Gaiety Theatre, the Prince did subsequently give her all the support she needed. She had the sort of public myth and magnetism that attracted him, and the close friend-

---

* In 1895, when the Rhodes-inspired Jameson Raid on Johannesburg backfired, earning Rhodes much criticism and unpopularity, the Prince proved the staunchest of his friends, continuing to invite Rhodes to Marlborough House and Sandringham throughout the crisis.

ship of the Prince of Wales virtually guaranteed her social and theatrical triumph on her future visits. On one occasion he employed his most serviceable of friends, Ferdinand de Rothschild, to give a midnight supper party in her honor at his great house in Piccadilly so that she could meet some of the leading lights of high society and be presented to the Duc d'Aumale. Another time he set the tongues wagging by visiting a French Fete at the Albert Hall where Bernhardt was managing a stall. Lillie Langtry was also there, but Bertie apparently spent much more time and money with "the Divine Sarah" than with the Jersey Lily, and one of Sarah Bernhardt's biographers detects a possible "air of the boudoir" about the note she sent to her manager in June 1880— "I've just come back from the Prince of Wales. It is twenty past one. I can't rehearse any more at this hour. The Prince has kept me since eleven." What happened in the boudoir scarcely matters, and the self-proclaimed greatest actress in the world always treated mere fleshly matters as totally subsidiary to her art.* What counted was that Bertie, the man of fashion, was enjoying the public notoriety of friendship with the most vaunted actress of the age, and it was in 1883, when she was playing *Fédora* in Paris, that this friendship brought him its unique reward. Visiting the actress in her dressing room, he happened to remark that he had always secretly longed to be an actor. She took him at his word and next night at the climax of the play when Fédora discovered the corpse of her lover Vladimir and wept beside his deathbed, few people in the audience realized that the "corpse" was none other than the Prince of Wales, who was finally achieving his childhood ambition.

---

* On one occasion an admirer who had paid a vast sum to sleep with her found her awaiting him in bed made up as a toothless hag.

In fact Paris continued to be the one place where Bertie felt completely free. His sensual education had begun here after his marriage, and continued with the most famous courtesans of the Second Empire during the sixties. It had been in his honor that Cora Pearl was served up, naked beneath an enormous silver cover, as the *pièce de résistance* of a banquet at the Café Anglais. And also at the Café Anglais he first met the tempestuous La Barucci, famous for her Roman eyes and queenly bearing, and for the way she would dramatically declaim with strong Italian accent, *"Je souis la Vénous de Milo! Je souis la première putaine de Paris!"* Bertie had asked his elegant friend the Duke of Gramont-Caderousse to make the introduction, and the Duke, knowing La Barucci well, had gone to great lengths instructing her on how to show proper respect to the heir to the throne of England. Despite this she was inevitably late. Bertie as usual arrived at the appointment on the dot, and he and the Duke found themselves waiting for the famous beauty to appear. Finally, a good hour late, La Barucci, regal and unapologetic, swept in to make her curtsy. She was in the height of fashion, wearing a décolleté dress and a transparent wrapper that revealed her splendid breasts and shoulders.

"Your Royal Highness," said the Duke, trying to make light of her rudeness before the Prince, "may I present the most unpunctual woman in France?"

The Prince smiled, but La Barucci was outraged at being reprimanded, even before the future King of England. Instead of replying she stood where she was, tossed back her head, then calmly dropped her diaphanous dress onto the floor. The Duke was horrified, but Bertie predictably amused.

"Voilà qui nous console de notre attente," he said, bowing towards the lady, and from all accounts from that moment

all was forgiven, with Bertie and *la première putaine de Paris* "the greatest friends in the world."*

But courtesans and chorus girls apart, Bertie was very much at home in the rarified and snobbish society of the Faubourg St. Germain. His friendships there managed to survive the death of the Empire and the establishment of the Republic in 1870—all this despite Bertie's close sympathies with the exiled Emperor and the Empress Eugénie. For as usual, where his pleasures were at stake, Bertie would not permit a silly point of principle to keep him from doing what he most enjoyed for long, and throughout the seventies Bertie continued with his life of fashionable Parisian rake as cheerfully under the Republican regime as ever he had during the Empire. More so if anything! For now that the Emperor's court at Fontainebleau was dead, Bertie became the nearest thing to real royalty to be found in France. *Le Prince de Galles* was considered very chic in Republican France. In October 1874 he was extravagantly entertained by the French President, the Republican Marshal MacMahon—who took him hunting at Marly—but that same autumn he was able to visit a number of his favorite Legitimist families as well, in almost equal style—the Rochefoucauld Bisaccias, the Duc de Chartres, his close friend the Marquis de Gallifet, and the Duc de Mouchy.

With friends like these, Bertie could enjoy much the same freedom of living off the stately homes of France as he had in England, and during the seventies he had developed what was virtually a duplicate round of pleasure across the Chan-

---

* One story, however, does tell how afterwards Gramont-Caderousse scolded her for her behavior. "Didn't you tell me to behave properly before the Prince?" she replied. "I showed him the best I have—and for free."

nel. Close friends like the Duc and Duchesse de Mouchy* and the rich and Anglophile M. and Mme. Standish stayed frequently at Marlborough House—and in return Bertie could always use their opulent Paris houses as his own. He also inevitably had his own aristocratic mistress in France—who soon assumed the unofficial role which Lillie Langtry simultaneously enjoyed in London, that of *maîtresse en titre* to the Prince of Wales. This was the banker's daughter, the sumptuous and willful Princesse de Sagan. Since Bertie first met her just before his marriage at the court of the Empress Eugénie at Fontainebleau, she had made a great marriage to the Prince de Sagan, a dandy and celebrated wit who also enjoyed the title and estates of Talleyrand-Périgord. They cordially disliked each other, but seem to have made the most of their antipathy, both taking countless lovers, both repeating malicious witticisms at each other's expense, and both becoming figures of high fashion in their different spheres.

She was exactly the sort of aristocratic mistress Bertie loved—hard, witty, and sufficiently experienced to ensure that no indiscretion or embarrassment marred their relationship. She seems to have treated her role as Bertie's mistress as something of a social honor and a semiroyal appointment —so did her husband, who thought it the height of fashion to be cuckolded by the Prince of Wales. Passion apart—and somehow one feels that with this banker's daughter, passion played far less part than calculation—the arrangement clearly suited Bertie. The lady was far too sensible to dream of demanding the exclusive attentions of the Prince, even if she

* Anna de Mouchy, a famous beauty of her day, was granddaughter of Napoleon's Marshal Joachim Murat, the innkeeper's son who became King of Naples. She was brought up a Protestant by her American mother (a Frazer of Baltimore), turned Roman Catholic, and was given an annual income of £40,000 by Napoleon III when she married Antoine de Noailles, Duc de Mouchy.

had wanted them, so that her role of princely mistress could cheerfully continue from 1867 until well into the eighties— with all the prestige that the post implied. At the same time Bertie was able to enjoy not just her ample favors, but also his favorite house in Paris, the magnificent Sagan mansion on the Rue St. Dominique. She also entertained him in the style to which he was accustomed at her enormous castle, Mello, to the south of Paris, and, come the spring, she would be ready to welcome him in the South at her beautiful estate at Cannes.

When he was with the aristocracy in France, Bertie was careful to insist on the full respect due to a future sovereign and a royal heir. Not that the royalist nobility often forgot it, but if they did Bertie knew how to remind them of their manners, as when on one occasion a rich host asked him if he would kindly ring the bell to summon a servant. Bertie did so, but only to call his carriage and leave immediately.

But Bertie enjoyed another life in Paris away from the formal world of the Faubourg St. Germain. More than in London he could enjoy the freedom of driving through the streets, attending the theatres, and dining out with a pretty woman like any rich man about town. Even at the height of his affair with Lillie Langtry, he used to feel it prudent to meet her in Paris when they wanted a few days together away from the public eye. And the queenly presence of the Princesse de Sagan in the Rue St. Dominique never inhibited him from visiting his actresses (Sarah Bernhardt was only one of the countless leading ladies whose dressing room he graced) or enjoying a night out at the Moulin Rouge. The first time this occurred, Zidler, the director of the Moulin Rouge, was for once tipped off in advance that *le Prince de Galles* would be arriving incognito. The result was panic. The whole place was spring-cleaned, fresh performers hired for the band, and all the dancers were on tenterhooks. For once Bertie was late. The hours ticked by, then sometime after midnight when Zidler had given up expecting him, the portly figure entered the theatre. Consternation ensued but La Goulue—the star of the Moulin Rouge immortalized in old age by Toulouse-Lautrec—saved the situation. With studied disdain for the Prince and his elegant friends, she slowly descended the stairway from the stage and then, just a few feet from the Prince, launched into the cancan. Bertie was delighted, the evening ended riotously, and from then on La Goulue became one of those special people from whom almost any familiarity was allowed. Not long afterwards he came to see her dancing at the Jardin de Paris. As he entered she paused, one leg in the air, and called out with her strong Parisian accent—"*Ohé Galles, tu paie le champagne.*" And for once, pay he did.

By the late eighties, the incessant visits and insatiable enjoyments of the Prince of Wales had made him something of a Parisian institution, a mainstay of the Paris season and one of the regulars at the Opéra, the Jardin de Paris, and even the shows of Montmartre. And inevitably stories were told about him and his amours. How true they are is anybody's guess, but they all bear the mark of a character whose love life has already entered popular mythology. Some of them concerned his affairs with dashing Americans like "Miss Emily X" and "la Belle Mademoiselle Fortescue," but the most interesting of them describe the love affairs he had with ordinary women of the streets, like the pretty middle-class woman he seduced in a private room of a restaurant near the Luxembourg. As the meal ended they discovered that the husband had followed his wife, and was waiting for her to reappear. The woman was in tears, but the Prince, resourceful as a popular hero should be, disguised the pretty Mme.

S . . . as a pastry cook, allowed her to escape unrecognized, and then asked the waiting husband if he would mind calling him a cab.

But one of the Prince's best apocryphal remarks dates from Paris at the end of the nineties when Bertie was staying at the Ritz. He was nearing sixty, and at the end of a long and splendid dinner turned to a friend and said, somewhat wearily, "You Frenchmen are always talking of your Eternal Father, but I can see that you don't know what it is to possess an Eternal Mother."

The Malady of Love

10

It says much for the Prince's energy and forthright nature that, as his fifties loomed, he was still plodding down his sexual highway as steadily as ever, never permitting himself to be diverted or delayed, phlegmatically enjoying each pleasure as it came, then belching gracefully, offering a signed photograph or modest jeweled souvenir, and waddling on towards the next night's conquest, wreathed in cigar smoke and his princely dignity.

His women were getting older now; all in their second wind of marriage, they had reached the point where husbands had grown tolerant or unconcerned. Within his social ambit he enjoyed a more or less acknowledged *droit de seigneur* which nobody resented. Such was his prestige within society that his embraces, however casual and brief, were regarded as a sign of godlike favor. Nobody commented adversely on his achievements as a lover. He was above that sort of feline gossip—and the boudoir honors of his all-too-solid presence were quite emphatically their own reward.

The Princess had long ago abandoned all attempt to restrain him, having learned by now that his infidelities were no threat to their marriage—or to her position in the public eye or in her family. Rather the reverse. The general public universally admired her for the tact and style with which she sustained her role, and one wonders just how much part Bertie's infidelities played in her unflagging popularity. For she was the professional wronged wife par excellence, never letting down her wayward husband in public, always superbly dressed and dignified, and limping slightly from the rheumatic fever she developed after the birth of her third child in 1867.

What she did in private is something of a mystery. As "Dearest Mother-dear" to the two Princes and the three Princesses, she had always ruled the nursery. Bertie, a tolerant and devoted father to his children, seems to have stood in something approaching awe of her, with her apparent artlessness, her unfading, slightly frigid beauty, and her unfailing rectitude. All her five children seem to have felt the same. Her most extraordinary achievement was to maintain an apparently platonic love affair with one of her husband's equerries for nearly a quarter of a century without a breath of scandal reaching the public or a whiff of jealousy bothering her marriage. This was the handsome and far from cold-blooded Captain Oliver Montagu, who was her confidant and friend, her constant partner in the balls at Marlborough House, and her *cavaliere servente* until the day he died. He was in constant attendance at Sandringham, and the Princess was obviously devoted and dependent. By all the rules of the Marlborough House "set," they could and should have been long-established lovers, but it seems they were not. Perhaps sex was not important to the Princess after six pregnancies—and perhaps beneath the artlessness she had the sense to realize that once she lost her irreproachability she would lose her public image and her hold on Bertie. Things suited her exactly as they were.

It was against this background that the Prince, now in his forty-ninth year, did something unexpected. For the first time in his life, he fell totally and more or less subserviently in love. Perhaps this was predictable. In all his love affairs as Prince of Wales he had been firmly in command, always the dominating partner in each relationship, always the one who could decide when *he* had had enough and it was time to move on. Now, after thirty years of dedicated womanizing, he had found his match—the woman who would not grate-fully submit to His Royal Highness's pleasure and who, when she did become his mistress, always loved him rather less than he loved her.

This most unusual woman was Daisy, Countess of War-wick. She was born in 1861 in a house in Berkeley Square as the nation mourned the death of the father of her future lover—Albert the Prince Consort. She always claimed to be descended on one side from Nell Gwyn and on the other from Oliver Cromwell—and certainly throughout her life she combined the amorous success and beauty of the one with the resoluteness of the other. Her father, Charles Maynard, was a colonel in the Blues and son of the wealthy Viscount Maynard. He was tall, good-looking, and energetically eccen-tric. On one occasion at a bullfight in Spain he leaped on the bull's back, galloped it round the ring, and was nearly lynched. He died when she was three, her grandfather made her his heir, and as a very young child she became one of the richest heiresses in the country. Her widowed mother had remarried—to the Earl of Rosslyn—and the house they lived in, Easton Lodge, soon became her property. To add to the drama of her childhood, there was even a period when she had to be accompanied by a burly manservant for fear of abduction by hostile members of the family. From such a background of wealth, tragedy, and eccentricity, the young Miss Maynard soon developed into something of a character. "She is beautiful as she is good," reported the *Essex Herald* loyally when she was just seventeen, "and she has £30,000 a year. The photographers are pursuing her, august dressmakers in Belgravia are praying to her to give them patronage, and a fashionable bootmaker in Regent Street has even named a new heel after her."

But Daisy Maynard was not very anxious to be photographed and turned into one more glossy society beauty. She was already very much the aristocrat, with a mind of her own, and far more interested in horses than society. But the fact that she was an heiress could not be overlooked, and before long her near-neighbor, Disraeli, was suggesting her to Queen Victoria as a prospective wife for her younger son, Prince Leopold. (Victoria by now had finally abandoned the idea of marrying her children off to continental royalty in favor of suitably rich home-grown commoners.) Victoria accepted the idea, invited Daisy to dine at Windsor, and thoroughly approved of her. But when Daisy met the Prince, the plan went wrong. Instead of him, she immediatly fell in love with his equerry, Lord Brooke. Prince Leopold, it seems, was rather grateful, as he was already in love with someone else, and although Victoria was disappointed at not having Daisy for her daughter-in-law, she did not push the match, agreeing that without love, "the divinest thing in the world," no marriage could possibly succeed.

Daisy was to remain on close terms with the Queen and

Royal Family. As she wrote, many years later, "I was a 'beauty,' and only those who were alive then know the magic that word held for the period. I was physically fit, eighteen, unspoilt, and I adored dancing." And in 1880, still aged eighteen, the beauty married "Brooky" in Westminster Abbey, with Prince Leopold as best man and the Prince and Princess of Wales as guests of honor. By Victoria's command the bride and groom were invited to Windsor next day so that the Queen could see Daisy in her wedding dress.

In Lord Brooke Daisy had chosen herself the ideal husband. He was eminently presentable, the Earl of Warwick's eldest son, educated at Eton and a military academy, and a conservative M.P. since 1879. He was not dangerously intelligent, which might have led to competition with his formidable young wife; instead he had shown his mettle by leaving Oxford without a degree, to become one of the best shots in the country. He was content and kind and tolerant, "a perfect gentleman" as his wife said later. It was as well that he was, for Lord Brooke, later the fifth Earl of Warwick, was already cast by fate to be the most eminent cuckold of his generation.

Daisy entered into married life with gusto, and by her twentieth birthday seemed quite set to be a *grande dame* of the old school. She and her shootin'-fishin' husband were invited everywhere—including Sandringham and Windsor. Some hint of the opulence of the period is given in her memoirs, where she describes how she and her husband were invited to a fox hunt in Normandy by the French Rothschilds. The English Rothschilds had shown their usual family solidarity by lending a pack of foxhounds—from Sir Nathaniel's kennels at Tring—and the French huntsmen's scarlet coats had been cut specially for the occasion by a leading English tailor. (The ordinary hunt servants were in green and gold.)

The French sportsmen seem to have been distinctly shaken by the hunt before the dashing Lady Brooke arrived. Large notices with "Danger" on them had been placed by all the jumps and there were already several walking wounded among the guests. This was just the situation that she loved. Danger and excitement were her element, and for the next few days she showed the Rothschilds how to hunt as she hurtled across the countryside, ignoring the danger signs and never drawing rein at any hazard.

She conducted her life in much the same breathless style. Everything at full pelt! When she decided she would like to see Land's End she drove the three hundred miles from Easton in her coach nonstop, with teams of horses specially sent down from Ward's of London. When bicycles became the rage she bought the first one in the district and pedaled off in all directions. When she grew bored with Easton, she had the whole façade promptly redesigned.

The same impatience and highhandedness ruled her private life. She had a son by Lord Brooke in 1882, but despite this, and despite her husband's gentlemanliness and unmatched skill with rod and gun, she felt she needed the amorous equivalents of hedges to jump and foxes to pursue. There was no difficulty finding them. Her weekend parties at Easton became notorious. They were exclusive, intimate, and often as dramatic as their hostess. She would invite members of the international aristocracy and young bloods from her father's old regiment, and began moving in a hothouse atmosphere of love affairs and brisk flirtations. She was quite frank about it all and totally without remorse. As she wrote calmly in old age, "I could not help it. They were there. It was all a great game."

This was the point where Lord Brooke's gentlemanly qualities came to the fore. He shot compulsively. He avoided scenes. And like that other badly savaged husband, Mr. Langtry, he spent long weekends indulging in the favorite sport of cuckolds—fishing. But unlike Langtry—who after all was not a gentleman—Lord Brooke did somehow manage to maintain a sort of friendship with his wife. On one occasion she was in Paris and heard that a current lover had been killed—how else?—in a hunting accident. Disturbed by the news, she broke her holiday, and stepped off the boat at Dover to find Lord Brooke there to meet her. "I knew you'd be upset," he said, "and thought I'd better come."

Such a saintly understanding seems to have saved the marriage—but it could not prevent Daisy from finally becoming entangled with the Prince of Wales. Considering his tastes and her availability, it is surprising that it took so long, especially as he had known her since her teens. Perhaps he discerned the danger signs. There had been sufficient tempests in his life without inviting trouble from a female hurricane. But then, in 1889, the inevitable occurred, and true to form, the thirty-year-old Daisy Brooke entered his life trailing disaster and destruction in her wake.

The start of the affair was sufficiently unusual and involved to have given Bertie all the warning that he needed, but possibly he found the sheer complexity of her affairs appealing, as rakes do when the ease of conquest has made life a little tedious.

In 1883, Daisy had become involved with Bertie's friend and fellow rake, a rumbustious Irishman and gallant sailor, Lord Charles Beresford, who encouraged her fast tastes and headlong horsemanship by giving her lessons in driving a four-in-hand. To start with, Lady Beresford was included in the invitations to Easton, but soon he was coming on his own, and before long was conducting not just the coach, but a passionate romance with its owner. Beresford was an accomplished womanizer, and the following year became a popular hero as well by organizing transport steamers up the Nile to relieve Gordon at Khartoum.* On his return to Easton, Daisy greeted him with open arms and a firework display. Rings were exchanged, protests of undying love were sworn, and when a child was born Daisy had him christened Charles.

The Prince had known what was going on—and treated it all with tolerant amusement. He liked to see his friends enjoy themselves. But by 1888 Lord Charles's passions, always fickle, had begun to cool, and the next year he quietly returned to active service. Daisy, however, was more in love than ever. Her pride was injured, and the last straw came when she went on holiday to the Riviera only to meet Lord Charles and his lady wife. Lady Charles was all too obviously *enceinte.*

With Lady Charles's looks (and steadfast morals) there was no question but that her husband was the father. For Daisy this was intolerable. After the rings they had exchanged, the vows they had sworn, she still regarded Lord Charles as her property. How dare he commit what amounted to adultery—especially with his wife. This was the gist of an historic letter which she penned him in the height of jealousy and passion. Unfortunately for everyone involved, before it could reach its proper destination it was opened by the pregnant Lady Charles, who became even more outraged than the outraged Daisy. First she complained to the great Lord Salisbury about Lady Brooke's intolerable goings-on. Lord Salisbury was understandably baffled, and had nothing to suggest, so Lady Charles reached promptly for her solicitor, and sent the offending letter off to him.

---

* It was at the Battle of Abu Klea, when all the other naval officers were killed, that Lord Charles Beresford made the remark that it would be "hard to die without knowing who had won the Derby."

The famous solicitor, George Lewis, is a key figure in the social history of the period. According to Daisy herself he was the "ever ready friend" of Bertie's circle and of high society. A man of infinite discretion and countless secrets, he was the supreme smoother and fixer of his day. He specialized in settling divorces out of court and with the minimum of public scandal—a service which naturally endeared him to the Prince. The full story of what he did for Bertie and for several hundred of his eminent clients in this direction will never be known. But on this one occasion when he had to deal with the frantic Lady Beresford, his fine discretion seems to have deserted him. The fixer made the situation worse.

He began by informing Daisy that he had her most compromising letter in his safe—presumably with the aim of scaring her and getting an apology. But Daisy was difficult to scare, and instead of knuckling under she sought help from the most influential source she knew—the Prince of Wales.

Bertie was moved by Daisy's plight and beauty. He also called on Lewis and ordered him to show him the offending letter. This he did, but when Bertie tried to make him destroy it there and then, Lewis jibbed at such unprofessional behavior, and promptly sent the letter back to Lady Beresford. By now the Prince was clearly under Daisy's spell. Adopting his sternest role of "social despot," he tried using all his influence to persuade Lady Beresford to destroy the letter—again without result—and when the lady persisted in refusing his request, he banished her from the invitation list of Marlborough House, an action which was tantamount to social ostracism.

Throughout these heady goings-on, Bertie had placed himself still further in the wrong by taking the future Lady

Warwick to his bed. Whatever feelings she still had for faithless Beresford were soon forgotten in the embraces of the Prince, and he, in turn, had now become a committed protagonist for his new dynamic mistress. It all sounds very pretty, but the Aylesford scandal should have warned the Prince of what could happen when jealousy and emotions all get out of hand. Instead of calming everybody down, he seems to have become so influenced by the demanding Daisy that he was soon lined up against the embattled Lady Charles. Solicitor Lewis was invited several times to Sandringham in the good cause. The social embargo on Lady Beresford continued, and she retaliated by penning still more indignant letters to the still more baffled Prime Minister, Lord Salisbury. The gist of her complaint was that the Prince of Wales was "taking up the cause of an abandoned woman against that of a perfectly blameless woman like myself for gratification of his own private desires!!"—a charge which, give or take a little womanly exaggeration, was, broadly speaking, true.

But worse was still to come, as like some social snowball the row rolled on. Lord Charles became involved—his wife had begun to complain to him over the indignities inflicted on her by the Prince of Wales. By now she had given birth to the child who had started all the trouble, and her husband was obviously concerned at her distress. But the finer points of human nature were not his forte and he approached the whole affair just as he approached the enemy at Abu Klea. En route to the Mediterranean to take command of his new flapship, the *Undaunted,* he stopped off at Marlborough House to tell his old friend and future sovereign just what he thought of him.

There are several versions of what happened. According to one, Lord Charles pushed Bertie angrily onto a sofa and called him a blackguard and a coward. According to another he "came within an ace of striking the Prince with his fist." Still another version has Bertie backing nimbly from the aggressive Beresford and telling him not to strike him since such a move would inevitably be the end of Lord Charles's career and social standing. Certainly there were high words, the Prince was deeply insulted, and Lord Charles went off to his warship muttering black threats of wrath and revenge.

From then the trouble rumbled on throughout the year 1891, and past Bertie's fiftieth birthday in November of that year. The Prince continued, not unnaturally, to exclude Lady Beresford from invitations to Marlborough House. She grew increasingly hysterical at what was, in effect, a social boycott. And her warlike husband thundered intermittently at Bertie from the Mediterranean, threatening to reveal all to the press. As everybody knew, this was the real danger for, as in every princely fracas since the Mordaunt case, the monarchy itself was always put at risk by the threat of public scandal. A decorous affair with Lillie Langtry was one thing; a case like this, with Bertie behaving in so dubious a light, quite another.

Finally this danger was averted—just. But not before the Queen, the Princess of Wales, the Prime Minister, and Beresford's brother, Lord Marcus Beresford, had all been solemnly dragged in to make the Beresfords see sense and calm things down. Daisy's original offending letter was ultimately burned, the case was kept out of the newspapers, and Lord Charles went on to further glory in the Royal Navy.

But what is interesting about the episode is the way the pattern of all Bertie's previous misadventures seemed to repeat itself, once things had started getting out of hand. His wife was loyally invoked to back him up. The politicians had to rally round, and Queen Victoria herself, for all her constant disapproval of his choice of friends, stood loyally and effectively by him when disaster loomed. What is also interesting is that throughout the uproar and the outbursts, Bertie's affection for Daisy never wavered. Indeed, the only possible explanation for this inept behavior during the whole period is that the driving Daisy had completely conquered him.

Undoubtedly, from the beginning, she had enjoyed the high drama and excitement that surrounded the affair. She was just thirty; her beauty was at its height, and an affair with the Prince of Wales was something of a culmination after all her other loves. So she had entered into it with all her natural gusto and determination—and Bertie was quite bowled over. According to Daisy's biographer, Alexandra had realized this from the start, and whereas she had been quite tolerant of Lillie Langtry, "the affair with Lady Brooke promised to be altogether more turbulent, and in the early stages the Princess's sympathies naturally lay with Lady Charles. The Prince for his part, felt an adoration, protectiveness and lasting devotion towards Lady Brooke."

The press soon began hinting at what was going on. On May 6, 1891, a *World* reporter wrote with obvious innuendo —"At the opera, the Prince of Wales with his two youngest daughters. Lady Brooke was in the pit tier, and the writer craned his neck to catch a glimpse of the goddess whose fame had penetrated even to the dim recesses of the placid country. Her profile was turned away from the inquisitive world, but I made out a rounded figure, diaphanously draped, and a brilliant haughty, beautiful countenance."

So much for Daisy's looks: she had other means as well of keeping Bertie, and from the beginning of 1891 the Prince of Wales became a regular attender at Lady Brooke's house of love at Easton. There was a small stone summer house where they made love and in time—as if in proof of the permanency of their love—she built a special railway station near her home so that the Prince could steam up in his special train and their love would have to endure no delays. More sentimentally, they followed the old Easton habit of exchanging rings—the one from Bertie was inscribed inside, "to Bertie from his affectionate parents, A and VR, 9 July 1860." It was his confirmation ring. Once he had given it he called her his beloved "Daisy wife."

His love for Daisy presumably made all the troubles with the Beresfords appear worthwhile, but after so many years of cheerful rakishness, Bertie was suddenly accident-prone, and 1891 was to prove a year of near-disaster. For as well as all the Beresford affair, he had to face the public scandal that followed his stay at Tranby Croft.

This was the home of a shipowner called Arthur Wilson, and the previous September he had entertained the Prince and several of his close friends from the Marlborough House set during St. Leger week. In the evenings the party played the Prince's favorite game of baccarat,* and one of the guests, Sir William Gordon-Cumming, was twice seen cheating. Bertie was informed and with his agreement, Gordon-Cumming was persuaded to sign a paper promising that, in return for everybody's silence, he would never play cards again. Bertie kept the document and trusted that the unpleasant incident was over. But it was not. By the new year it was clear that somebody *had* talked, and the news of the Tranby Croft affair was round the London clubs.

It was in a belated attempt to clear his name that Gordon-Cumming brought a civil action against Bertie's five original friends who had made the accusation against him at Tranby Croft. When the case was heard before the Lord Chief Justice at the beginning of June, the Prince was automatically sub-

* At this time he used to carry his own counters with him, engraved with the Prince of Wales feathers, the gift of the Sassoons.

poenaed as a witness. This was the second time—the Mordaunt case was the first—that the heir to the throne had been in a court of law, and to the general public it naturally seemed as if he himself were standing trial. During the nine days the trial lasted, Bertie was in court every day but one, and the whole business, coupled with the Beresford worries, was clearly something of an ordeal, especially as Gordon-Cumming's counsel went out of his way to be offensive to the Prince. For one of the very few occasions in his life, Bertie knew what it was to spend a sleepless night.

Gordon-Cumming lost the case—and retired, a social outcast, to spend the remainder of his life with his freshly wedded American heiress. But Bertie was also something of a loser from the case. He felt the humiliation of having his private life dragged before the courts. There was a widespread feeling that Gordon-Cumming had been badly treated by his friends, and the idea of the Prince of Wales playing a sinful-sounding *foreign* game struck many people as the depths of depravity.*

It was one thing for the Prince to have an eye for an attractive woman. It was quite another for him to indulge in the hideous vice of gambling. The fact that the English, as a race, are probably the most inveterate gamblers in the world hardly came into it, and once again, as if to show the thinness of the ice on which he trod, Bertie was caught by a sudden creaking of unpopularity, similar to that which followed the Mordaunt case.

Once again a princely "scrape" seemed to have illogically

* There were also rumors that Gordon-Cumming had been made the scapegoat for someone else at Tranby Croft, the imputation being that the someone was the Prince himself. It is these rumors which have continued to this day to give credence to the idea that there was much more to the scandal than ever emerged. There is, however, not a scrap of evidence to support this thesis.

outraged the earnestness and puritanism of the country. And once again Bertie's rakish habits seemed to be endangering the throne. The press weighed in: the *Times* itself expressed the hope that Bertie, like the wretched Gordon-Cumming, would also sign a pledge against playing cards. And even Victoria, in an attempt to calm the public feeling against the Prince, tried to persuade him to write a public letter to Archbishop Benson condemning gambling as a social event.

Whatever else he may have been, the Prince was not a hypocrite—and emphatically declined. His letter of refusal, though, is interesting since it gives his views, as an experienced man of the world and long-established rake, on the whole subject of gambling. As one might have expected, he took a tolerant and common-sense view, arguing that betting or playing cards for money was not what he called gambling. These only became gambling—a "vice" for which he said he professed the greatest horror—when they were done for stakes which people could not afford, or when the betting turned into a compulsive habit. As he wrote to the Archbishop, "I have a horror of gambling, and should always do my utmost to discourage others who have an inclination for it, as I consider that gambling, like intemperance, is one of the greatest curses that a country can be afflicted with."

A further worry for the Prince that summer was his eldest son, Prince Edward, Duke of Clarence, who at the age of twenty was appearing distinctly like his father—only more so. He combined extraordinary backwardness at work with still more extraordinary forwardness with women. Eddy had failed consistently at military academy and also got himself mixed up with women of low company. In this he never showed any of his father's tact or sense of discretion or decorum. Unlike his younger brother George—a stalwart lad and great favorite of his father's—Eddy was such a menace that the Prince was in despair. His irresponsibility and near-idiocy were such that if news of them got out the future of the British Royal Family would look grim indeed. A rakish heir was bad enough; when he in turn possessed a son like Eddy there could not be much hope for the continued popularity of monarchy in Britain. Bertie was keen to banish him—in true Victorian style—on a long, absorbing tour of the colonies, but he was hardly in the position to play the heavy father. Interestingly enough, it was Alexandra who appeared more understanding. Perhaps she knew far less about what he had been up to, but thanks to her, Bertie agreed to let him stay in England with his regiment and then become engaged to young Princess May of Teck the following spring. As in his own case, thirty years before, it was felt that all that the young man needed was a wife.

One feels that Bertie was not built for worries, and all the tensions of that summer must have made Daisy and her idyllic house at Easton doubly alluring. Bertie was continually there. Each weekend Daisy would triumphantly send out her invitations with the magic words—"to meet H.R.H. the Prince of Wales." And with this middle-aged affair with a woman twenty years his junior Bertie was suddenly revealing a new and unsuspected self—a demanding and sentimental lover. Daisy was very much in command. The Prince would dutifully appear with her on more and more public occasions—at church, at the races, and even after the theatre at their favorite restaurants in London: Rules in Maiden Lane, the Cafe Royal, and Kettner's, where there is still an "Edward" room.

But it was in private that the real change appeared in Bertie. Gone was the practiced womanizer, the overindulged and sated rake. Instead there was a lover, constantly demanding all his mistress's time and reassurance during the worries of that troubled summer. This seems to have continued throughout their love affair. According to Daisy's memoirs, the Prince wrote to her two or three times a week, and complained bitterly if she did not reply immediately. "He needed an outlet for his superabundant emotions. So at times he was unusually sentimental. . . . For this reason he adored anniversaries, Christmases etc," and he chose all the presents that he gave her for careful sentimental reasons.

The disturbing novelty of a lovesick Bertie continued to disturb the Princess, so that on top of all the other troubles of the year 1891, there was also gossip that the Wales's marriage was in danger—especially when Alexandra stayed longer than usual with her parents in Copenhagen, and then, instead of coming home, moved on to the Crimea for a holiday with her sister, the Empress of Russia.

The patience of Daisy's saintly husband was also near its end, and it is said that at this crisis only the stern refusal of his father, the old Earl of Warwick, to allow the family name into the divorce courts saved the marriage. "The noble husband," *Truth* wrote in 1892, "acted as he always had done, with consummate good taste, the end being that the curious have been deprived of hearing the details of a case which, if not 'naughty,' was eminently piquant."

Piquant or naughty, the affair rolled on. The crisis in Bertie's marriage was averted when the unfortunate Prince Eddy, at the start of 1892, contracted influenza, then pneumonia, and died. The shock brought the parents back together. Alix was "wonderful." Sentimental Bertie wept. "Gladly would I have given my life for his," he wrote to his mother, and for a while it seemed as if he too had finally succumbed to that maudlin grief that was the real curse of the Coburgs. But not for long. Relations were restored with Alexandra—but this did not mean that he was any the less keen on Daisy. Soon they were off to Paris for a visit which she always claimed as one of the happiest memories of her life. She and her sister traveled with Bertie and his equerry, and together the four of them seem to have done Paris in style—all the new plays, a farce at the Palais Royal, a supper party at the Comédie Française given by the great Coquelin in their honor. Just to show that there were absolutely no marital hard feelings, Lord Brooke was permitted to join the party a few days later, and it was with him that they climbed the Eiffel Tower. But it was with the Prince alone that Daisy went through the small door in M. Eiffel's private room and completed the last climb to the very top.

In 1894 the old Earl of Warwick died—thus giving Daisy the title of Countess of Warwick, as well as the use of Warwick Castle and an abundant fortune. But this event also, indirectly, provided the next unexpected twist to her romance with the Prince. For it was the ball she gave at Warwick Castle that December which roused the ire of the socialist journalist Robert Blatchford. The ball was a very grand affair indeed, with special trains to Warwick Castle, a gold and white color scheme throughout the grounds, and masses of arum lilies specially rushed up from the South of France. Daisy, with some appropriateness, went dressed as Marie Antoinette.

Next day, to her fury, she read Blatchford's biting criticism of the whole affair and immediately dashed down to London to meet him in person and convince him of the unfairness of his attack. But she was to be the one who was convinced. Blatchford argued that the cost of the ball, while certainly providing employment, was ultimately unproductive—and therefore indefensible. Daisy reluctantly agreed.

Her conversion to socialism was as headlong as her hunting and her adulteries. Another strong influence on her was W. T.

Stead, the pioneer socialist and editor of the weekly *Review of Reviews,* who before long was suggesting that Daisy should use her influence on the heir to the British throne to positive effect.

For some time Daisy continued to combine her socialism and role as passionate *grande dame.* Elinor Glyn, who saw her around this time, wrote that, although she had seen the most beautiful and famous women in the world, "I have never seen one who was so completely fascinating as Daisy Brooke. . . . Hers was the supreme personal charm which I later described as 'It,' because it does not depend upon beauty or wit, although she possessed both in the highest degree."

By now, too, her Easton parties had become a legend. Again to quote from her biographer, "extra-marital relations flourished in the seductive surroundings. On arrival there was an afternoon tea, giving the men a chance to see who was there. After dinner he would have his first chance to move towards the lady of his choice. Propriety in public had to be observed and though a lady might be sitting next to her lover or lover-to-be, neither gave the slightest sign of this. The household routine was specially 'designed to facilitate little attentions pregnant with meaning.' Candlesticks were provided on a tray in the hall even if you didn't need one. Perhaps in lighting it for you an admirer might suggest a rendezvous. Otherwise notes were carefully placed on breakfast trays, and maids and valets involved in planning meetings."

This was the sort of world that Bertie loved—and she could offer. And offer it she continued to do for five more years—five years in which the Prince, if not entirely faithful, was at any rate more hers than he had ever been with any other woman.

When the romance finally began to fade—as all romances

did where Bertie was involved—it happened very slowly, and does not seem to have been entirely his fault. Part of the trouble was undoubtedly Daisy's increasing preoccupation with her international socialism. Like many wealthy idealists, she saw no reason why her beliefs had to conflict with her possessions. But an increasing proportion of her energies began to go now into her carefully planned good works— the technical and science school she was planning near Dunmow, the women's agricultural scheme at Reading, the shop she opened in Bond Street to sell needlework from young girls from the workhouse.

At first she tried to carry the Prince with her in these projects—and incredibly, to some extent she did. He visited the workhouse with her, had tea with Stead (where they discussed Cecil Rhodes), and according to Daisy, "I did everything that was in my power to let him know the truth about such places as workhouses and prisons, and I told him all I knew of the poor whom he would one day govern. In all this the Prince was a willing learner."

And so he may have been, but he remained an unrepentant and convinced conservative.

Then gradually Daisy herself began to change. Several bad hunting accidents kept her away from London, and it seems probable that after 1896, the relationship became increasingly platonic. Her pregnancy and the birth of her son, Maynard, in 1898 finally ended the affair. But despite this, she and the Prince remained close friends for several years to come, and it was during her pregnancy that she finally made her peace with Alexandra. She wrote Bertie a long letter in which she called Alexandra an "angel of goodness" and said she feared that enemies might have poisoned her mind against her. Bertie replied that he was delighted to be able to say that all was forgiven and that Alexandra would be happy to receive her once again. "She really quite forgives and condones the past, as I have corroborated what you wrote about our friendship having been platonic for some years. You could not help, my loved one, writing to me as you did—though it gave me a pang—after the letters I have received from you for nearly nine years!"

In fact, the Prince and Lady Warwick continued to correspond until his death, but just two weeks after this exchange of letters he met a married lady called Alice Keppel; and the final chapter in his sentimental journey had begun.

Rake's Haven

11

The Queen had passed quietly away at Osborne at 6:30 in the evening of January 22, 1901, in the arms of her frequently rebellious but now tearful grandson, the Kaiser. The Prince of Wales was also at her deathbed: her last utterance a softly murmured "Bertie!" And Bertie, at last, it was. Forty years, almost to the day, since his father died, the Prince had come into his inheritance.

His first act as sovereign seemed designed to assert his independence from the past. He had been christened Albert Edward, and as Victoria had emphasized before she died, it was King Albert Edward that she intended him to be. "It was beloved Papa's wish as well as mine that you should be called by *both* when you became king." The new King thought otherwise, and that first evening of his reign he made it plain that, despite his mother's wishes, he would rule by the single name of Edward.

This in itself seemed ominous and now that this sixty-year-old royal rake had finally made it to the throne, the question was just what sort of king he would turn out to be. There were some who felt a sense of real foreboding. The *Times,* in its accession leader, primly referred to things in the new king's long career "which those who respect and admire him could wish otherwise," and how, across the years, he had been "importuned by temptation in its most seductive forms."

But the mood of the new century was all for change, and the new king appeared to be immensely popular. The Kaiser's "vain old peacock" had slowly been transformed into what one French newspaper had christened "the uncle of Europe," and it was as a very worldly uncle, salacious, self-indulgent, and at last quite lovable, that his people greeted him.

Those intermittent fears which had plagued his mother during his years of waiting—fears that his scandalous behavior might actually impair the throne—had proved quite groundless. True, there had been some close shaves. But thanks to luck and to some help from his friends and from Victoria and her ministers at times, he had weathered all the scrapes and scandals of his forty years' rake's progress to the throne. Now, at last, the memory of his past was if anything a source of popularity. If, as the *Times* had put it, he had known "temptation in its most seductive forms," good luck to him! After six long decades of strictly moral monarchy, there was a feeling that a period of royal enjoyment and frivolity would hardly come amiss.

More important still, during the last few years before Victoria died, the Prince had finally become publicly accepted, warts and all, for the rake he was, a crowned Silenus, a genial cross between Priapus and John Bull.

This acceptance of his rakish public image had been a slowish process. It really started in the 1880's with his association with highly popular Mrs. Langtry, gathered momentum with Sarah Bernhardt, took quite a setback during the Tranby Croft scandal, and reached its zenith at the time of his accession. The whole process obviously owed much to the relaxed moral climate of the nineties. Another factor was undoubtedly the Prince's age. It was Somerset Maugham who pointed out the way the British venerate their grand literary old men. They also love their grand dirty old men. At a certain stage this curious process of apotheosis starts and the rake, who previously has been quite unacceptable, is suddenly transformed into a sort of public hero, a monument to the sheer durability of male potency.

The other element in the Prince's acceptance had been his success in certain fringe activities commonly associated with the rakish life. His sailing had been one of these. Ocean yacht racing is hardly a popular pastime, but the Prince's annual appearances at Cowes aboard his yacht *Britannia* drew him extraordinary popular acclaim. Even his shooting exploits, faithfully recorded by the press, were earning him a reputation as a "sportsman." But his greatest popularity undoubtedly came in the late nineties from his successes on the turf.

He had owned a racing stable since the sixties and always been a most enthusiastic betting man and student of the racing scene. But it was not until the year 1896 that he enjoyed a sudden vast success when his horse Persimmon, running at odds of five to one, won him the Derby. The scene on Epsom Downs as he led in his winner was a great demonstration of his ascending popularity, with an enthusiastic crowd bursting past the police to pat his back and roaring, "Good Old Teddy!" That night, at Marlborough House, he entertained the Jockey Club to a banquet, managed a midnight supper afterwards with the Countess of Dudley, and finally rolled off to bed with senses satisfied and his ambition splendidly fulfilled.

This period really did mark a new stage in his life. Until now he had never been completely sure of his public. They had turned on him at moments of personal disaster in the past, but this was no longer very likely. He had crossed the subtle line between the vulnerable and therefore private rake, and the acknowledged public figure who is accepted only for what he is. As Lord Granville wrote, "the Prince of Wales is loved because he has all the faults of which the Englishman is accused."

All of this plainly assisted him at his accession, and after half a century Albert's great system of producing the ideal royal heir was paradoxically succeeding. By sheer reaction, Albert had made his son a rake, and now a rakish king was what the people wanted. His clothes, his manner, had become a cult admired and imitated outside the narrow confines of society as in the past, and for his subjects there was vicarious pleasure in applauding this happy hedonist whose aim in life was still quite plainly to enjoy himself as much as possible.

Because of this, there was no need for sad renunciations of old friends and mistresses and happy pastimes now that he was King. This was no story of Prince Hal foreswearing pleasure once he had reached the throne. Life could go on for him almost as it always had—almost, but not quite. The incognito expeditions which he had always loved plainly had to cease, particularly those to France. Now that he was King he could hardly disappear for those carefree few days in Paris every spring under the title of the Earl of Chester. In fact, for several years now he had been steadily becoming something of a headache to the French police. During the nineties his face was too well known to let him wander off at will without police protection. The Prince had naturally objected to this, and the chief of the Paris police, fearing some incident or even an assassination bid, had kept him shadowed by plainclothesmen. This had caused trouble. On one occasion a rendezvous between the Prince and a married woman at the Jardin des Plantes was ruined when he recognized a pair of gardeners as the same men he had seen sitting at the next table in a restaurant the night before. There had been several hilarious incidents like this, and now that he was King, the freedom which is the privilege of unknown subjects was behind him.

There is one touching story from this period about the actress Réjane, who had briefly been his mistress in Paris in the early nineties. Going to Denmark soon after his accession, Edward had passed her at some reception without acknowledging her. Next day she apparently received a diamond clip with a note which read—"with apologies from the King of England who is no longer the Prince of Wales."

But as far as his public life and style of living were concerned, King Edward *was* still very much the Prince of Wales—only rather more so. His court became extremely grand and ostentatious, with state balls, à la Marlborough House, replacing Victoria's staid and widowlike drawing-room receptions. Buckingham Palace—morgue-like and half-deserted under Victoria, was rapidly and splendidly refurbished. The friends who for years had made the Marlborough House set almost a byword for fast living now formed the nucleus for what has been called "the most colorful court since Charles II's." And predictably the ceremonial and gastronomic aspects of the monarchy were treated seriously. Here Edward was in his element. Parliament had voted him a cool half million to sustain his various expenses and establishments. It was not enough—what monarch's stipend ever is? But it enabled him at least to make his court the best dressed and the best fed (some said most overfed) in Europe.

Court etiquette predictably became increasingly important. Edward possessed the common touch, but as one perceptive biographer has pointed out, he was fundamentally "immensely royal, almost to the point of eccentricity," and there is something strangely anachronistic in the exaggerated protocol which flourished round him now. There was a touch of the Versailles of Louis XIV in the obsessions of these gilded courtiers with form and precedence, style and decorations. They were of course echoing Edward's own fascination in such subjects, for his whole reign is studded with anecdotes of luckless diplomats wearing the wrong ribbon with some foreign order, or ladies who incurred the royal wrath by dressing unsuitably for dinner. One unfortunate society lady at a Buckingham Palace ball tripped over her train and fell flat on her face before the King. Instead of making Edward laugh, it infuriated him to have the dignity of a royal occasion upset by such a *faux pas*. She was never invited to the Palace again. And when Lord Rosebery arrived at Windsor wearing plain trousers instead of prescribed court dress of breeches and black stockings, the King was even less amused. "I presume," His Majesty said caustically, "that you have come in the suit of the American Ambassador."

The King could not overlook such solecisms, and in a wider sense this concern of his with detail and appearances reflects his whole concept of the monarchy. He was essentially concerned with the façade—the glittering reception, the turnout of a parade, the pantomime of royalty. A lifetime's rakishness and pleasure-seeking had left him largely unconcerned with deeper matters, and he was bringing the essential hedonist's philosophy to the kingship. Unlike his mother, he was not bothered in the least by anybody's morals, provided they avoided open scandal—and inevitably this attitude of his now became the keynote of smart Edwardian society. It was a rakish world, very much after Edward's heart—glossy and rather greedy and concerned with form, a bustling, empty, money playground for the extremely rich.

There was no great harm in this. Indeed it could be argued that the King's combination of wide popular appeal and a strictly deferential, plutocratic, and socially orientated court was an adroit formula for the monarchy during a time of change. A royal rake was what the country—and the monarchy—required. It would enable—as in fact it did—the effortless transition from the still strong personal monarchy of Queen Victoria to the cosmetic monarchy of Britain today.

But once again, there is a curious irony here, as far as Edward is concerned. For it is clear that none of this was quite what he intended. All of his adult life he had been waiting for real power, trying to see inside those red ministerial boxes, hoping to be consulted, longing to be "of use." In life Victoria had always blocked him, and now in death it seemed that she had beaten him again. For forty years she had been insisting he was too frivolous for power, and now that she had finally departed it was quite clear that she had taken with her the substance of her personal authority. All she had left her son was as much of the shadow as he could grasp.

It wasn't much. Victoria's iron grip upon events and politicians had depended on a lifetime's dedicated desk work and involvement in the daily stuff of politics. For the new King to have attempted this would have meant a total reconstruction of his life style, the abandoning of almost everything that he enjoyed. At twenty-five he might have managed it. At sixty it was inconceivable. He did try in an odd, haphazard way. In an attempt to emulate his mother's hours at her desk, he decided that he would personally sign all the commissions for his officers in the army and navy. (The task defeated him, and before long he was authorizing his secretary to employ a rubber stamp.) And apart from such eccentric acts, the bulk of his efforts to perform his kingly duties was not so very different from what he had grown used to while Prince of Wales—still more foundation stones to lay, more public libraries to open, and naturally those ever-present "social duties" were as pressing now as ever.

As might have been expected, he took immense pains planning the minutiae of what should have been the greatest moment of his life—his coronation, set for June 26, 1902—drawing up guest lists, deciding on points of precedence, helping design new livery for palace flunkeys, and setting the arrangements for the horde of foreign royalty who were invited. And as might also have been expected, fate's banana skin was waiting for him once again—this time in the form of an acute attack of appendicitis (then still a serious affliction) which struck him on the very eve of the great event.

The coronation had been planned as something of a jamboree of international royalty, with the heirs to almost every throne in the world ready to troop into Westminster Abbey at the solemn moment. Most of them had already arrived in London—His Imperial Highness Yi Chai-Kak of Korea, Grand Duke Michael of Russia, Said Ali of Zanzibar, Ras Makunan of Ethiopia, and Mohammed Ali Pasha of Egypt, quite apart from almost every crown prince in Europe. But Edward was not himself. For some months now he had been increasingly irritable. By mid-June the royal doctor, Sir Francis Laking, had had the temerity to diagnose appendicitis and, worse still, to attempt to put his royal master on a diet of milk and precious little else. Laking suggested an operation and, inevitably, the postponing of the coronation. The King wouldn't hear of it. When he missed Ascot, Laking informed the press that the King was suffering from lumbago. Final preparations for the coronation went inexorably ahead. The King grew worse. His temperature increased, his spirits sank. "If this goes on," he told Laking, "I shall give it up. I shall abdicate." But still there was no question of canceling the coronation. Edward told Laking manfully that he would see it through, even if he dropped dead during the attempt.

By June 23 it looked as though he would, for peritonitis had set in. Finally, in considerable pain, Edward agreed to the operation—and postponing the event for which he had waited almost forty years. The dress rehearsal for the coronation was hurriedly changed into a service of intercession just as the King slipped under the anesthetic. And the coronation had to wait six weeks until the principal performer—six inches thinner round the waist but otherwise no worse for the ordeal—was fit to make the journey to the Abbey and be crowned at last.

But though he was finally crowned as King and Emperor of the largest empire in the world, Edward's life did not really change. It was as necessary to keep the King amused as it had been to please the Prince of Wales. Boredom was still the greatest enemy. He was still restless if confronted with an empty day, and his diversions remained what they had always been—travel, society, food, and women.

Each spring he and Queen Alexandra would go cruising in the royal yacht named, without unconscious humor, the *Victoria and Albert.* This great steam-yacht with its gilt stateroom, its Marines' Band and scarlet-liveried flunkeys, its gold plate and galley which produced a flow of elaborate meals, was the floating epitome of Edwardian luxury. It had a crew of three hundred, and thirty court servants, and whenever the King was aboard his personal chef, the famed M. Ménager, was always there as well, supervising the soufflés, the ortolans, the game pies and lark puddings. And every summer Edward would be off *en garçon* for his statutory cure. Homburg had passed from fashion. The new place was Marienbad, the small Bohemian spa which Edward himself had done much to make fashionable, a great meeting place for the rich demi-monde of Europe; and although a lot of wealthy and fashionable English visitors followed their king there every summer (including Campbell-Bannerman and the unlikely radical M.P. John Burns), life for Edward was still much what it had always been at the end of August—steam baths, high colonics, some sexual therapy, and gentle gambling. And croquet in the afternoons.

At Marienbad the King could work off part of the accumulation of a whole year's overeating—and also keep his carnal appetites in trim. Throughout his sixties he was to remain almost embarrassingly virile, and while at Marienbad there was a regular routine by which he made his assignations with royal gallantry and entertained his casual mistresses back at his hotel. It was discreet and popular and probably helped him to lose weight.

This was important, for the older he got, the more he seemed to eat. Despite that warning from his father forty years before, he really was extraordinarily greedy, devouring five good solid meals a day (for the King, tea and supper both stood as full repasts) and sometimes, like Pooh Bear, finding the space for "a little something," say a lobster salad, in the morning.

More than ever, people noted the King's "intense enjoyment of good food," his love of caviar and ortolans, the way that he regarded grilled oysters as "the ideal supper dish," his passion for *Côtelettes de bécassines à la Souvaroff,* and his favorite way of eating pheasant, stuffed with woodcock which in turn were stuffed with truffles and served with a heavy sauce.

It is impossible to know how much his chronic overeating contributed to his moods of growing irritability and depression as his reign progressed. Probably a lot. Almost certainly the way he gulped such mountains of rich food—and smoked such quantities of large cigars—helped on his death. But as his reign progressed, one gets the feeling that, for all the unyielding pursuit of pleasure, he was no longer such a happy man as he had been while Prince of Wales.

His role as King did bring him certain triumphs—particularly abroad and particularly in France, where his celebrated royal state visit in the spring of 1903 helped pave the way for the *Entente Cordiale* signed between France and Britain the following year. It was in Paris that Edward the aging rake discovered a new role awaiting him—as Edward the Peacemaker, living symbol of the mood of understanding that was linking the two nations that he loved. His years of dedicated Gallic pleasure-seeking—the banquets, the affairs, the gambling, the titled mistresses—were paying a late dividend. At this moment when alliances were changing, the French were reassured and flattered by the presence of this English monarch who, with the tastes and manners of an old *boulevardier,* might almost have been one of themselves.

But elsewhere the King's conscientious efforts at diplomacy brought him little more than deep frustration. His attempts to influence the international power game through contacts with his royal relatives never had a chance. Diplomacy was too important to be left to kings, and in Germany he had the added irritation of the personal jealousy and venom of his nephew, the Kaiser. Edward's state visit to Berlin in 1909 seems to have reduced him to such a state of tension that at one point he had a seizure, fainted, and for some anxious moments was thought to be on the point of death. He recovered quickly and typically insisted on completing his appearances, but it was clear to everyone, including Edward, that his painful efforts had done nothing to improve the worsening relations between Britain and his nephew's government. Rather the reverse. The Germans were already using Edward as a symbol in their growing enmity with Britain, and his rakish reputation had made him vulnerable to German propaganda. Some of this certainly originated from the Kaiser personally. As early as Edward's coronation the story leaked out that the Kaiser had refused to allow the Crown Prince to attend for fear of the corrupting influence of Edward's court.* And from the beginning of his reign a campaign had started, part truth, but mainly cheap scurrility, to represent the King of England as an aging lecher, whose debauches typified the decadence of Britain.†

As the King's restlessness and irritation grew, and his periods of depression lengthened, his few close friends and family became increasingly important to him. His relations with Alexandra still had their squalls—given the circumstances it would have been unnatural if they had not. She refused to indulge in jealousy, as being an ignoble and, where

---

* The Kaiser had in fact been informed that during an earlier visit to England, the Crown Prince had disappeared from a ball attended by the Prince of Wales, and had been discovered in bed with one of the lady guests by Count Eulenburg, who had been delegated to look after him.

† Typical of these attacks on Edward's morals was *Der Prinz von Galles*, Sitten bilder *vom Königshofe* oder *Die Korruption in Hängland*, published anonymously in 1900. This highly colored fictional narrative purported to show the state of corruption around the heir to the English throne, and suggested that the Prince's choice of women was by no means confined to the courtesans of Paris. The story told of an expedition mounted by the Prince and several of his friends to abduct a beautiful French fishergirl from a village on the coast of France, in the royal yacht. Real-life characters like the Prince's friend, the Marquis de Gallifet, and the Princesse de Sagan were introduced into this entirely bogus story.

Edward was concerned, a pointless emotion. But this did not stop her showing her displeasure when a mistress seemed to be diverting Edward from his duties to his family. Similarly for him, her deafness must have been a source of irritation, and there were times when her chronic unpunctuality drove him to distraction. But despite this, there was an obvious affection between them which neither Edward's infidelities nor her infirmities could mar. Her looks were still virtually untouched by age, she performed her queenly duties with dignity and never-failing popularity, and he undoubtedly relied on her to keep the framework of his life in order.

Throughout his sixties, one of the few people whose continued presence never failed to delight him was his second son and now his heir, Prince George, the Duke of York. Between them there had grown a bond of genuine affection. Edward would be uneasy if a day passed without seeing him, and when the King died his son wrote, with evident sincerity, that he had lost "the best friend I have ever had."

Edward also had a few close cronies he relied on to divert him. One who became increasingly important was the extraordinary Marquis de Soveral, the Portuguese diplomat whose swarthy skin and simian features earned him the nickname of "the Blue Monkey." He was a raconteur and womanizer—two qualities that Edward always warmed to in a man—and this dapper, ugly little man was something of a fixture at court and an essential source of gossip and amusement.

Another friend the King relied on increasingly was the financier Ernest Cassel, now knighted and a Privy Councillor. Apart from his invaluable villa at Biarritz, where Edward spent several weeks each spring, Cassel possessed the Midas touch—and was always willing to employ it in his sovereign's service. There were continual rumors that he had "bought" his knighthood, and that he used to help Edward out of financial difficulties with unofficial gifts of money. Whether he did or not, he certainly assisted Edward with his investments and showed unerring skill in placing the royal money in high-yielding industrial stock. This was a necessary service, for the King was still incapable of living within his income. Inevitably Cassel enjoyed the royal favor.

The key figure of these last years of his life was without question his ultimate *maîtresse en titre,* the indomitable and quite extraordinary Mrs. George Keppel. When they first met in 1898 she was approaching thirty, and he was almost in his sixties, but she soon proved the perfect mistress for this evening king. Reading the memoirs of the period, one's first impression is of Mrs. Keppel's unshakable competence and tact. This even extended to the Queen—who liked her and who had the sense to be grateful for her influence upon her husband. She alone could calm him down when he was in a state, make sure that he enjoyed his evening's game of bridge, head off the dinner guests who bored him. She alone, of all his established mistresses, had the possibly disconcerting honor of being regularly invited with her husband to both Marlborough House and Sandringham.

The Honorable George Keppel, a younger son of the Earl of Albermarle, seems to have been another of the heroic Edwardian cuckolds. Exactly like the Earl of Warwick, he was a kindly, honorable aristocrat entirely overpowered by a sexier, younger, more ambitious and intelligent wife. Unlike the Earl of Warwick, the idea of divorcing his regally unfaithful wife never appears to have entered his patriotic head. The impression that one gets of this late romance is that those involved regarded it almost as a social duty rendered to the Crown. The King required his mistress just as he required his valet and his secretary, to say nothing of the hordes of courtiers and servants, cooks and flunkeys needed to keep his complex life in motion. She was the royal "friend" par excellence, and for once this most ambiguous of words seems to describe the essence of their relationship. Not that it was platonic—few relationships between Edward and the opposite sex ever were. But with remarkable energy and tact she filled the role which she created for herself. She became something of a buffer between the King and the world around him. Hostesses who wanted to ensure the good humor of their royal weekend guest would make sure to invite the omnipresent "Mrs. George" as well. Even the politicians and the civil servants would rely on her at times to reach the royal ear. Lord Hardinge, Edward's permanent head of the Foreign Office, paid tribute to her loyalty and tact and wrote of the occasions when he relied on her to present the Foreign Office view to Edward during their disagreements over policy.

She must have been extremely shrewd, for somehow she filled her eighteenth-century role of royal friend without arousing enmity or accusations of her undue influence or partiality.* Throughout the reign she maintained her unique position, did her duty, and kept an increasingly touchy and dyspeptic King in order. She was never jealous or possessive. That would have been impossible, for he remained as chronically promiscuous as ever, with his summer affairs at Marienbad and Paris, his regular liaisons with society women like Mrs. James and Mrs. Greville, and his unfailing eagerness to sample any fresh loveliness who caught his eye. The Honorable Mrs. George obviously learned much the same tolerance that Alexandra had adopted years before, and at the same

---

* Nor, it should be added, did she use her position for financial gain. It was the advice of Sir Ernest Cassel and her investments in Canadian stock that enabled her to buy her Italian villa, l' Ombrellino, where she retired in middle age.

time she managed to maintain her comfortable position with
the King. Each spring she would travel to Biarritz with him
for a week or two at Easter in Sir Ernest Cassel's villa. They
would walk along the dunes, gamble at little at the Casino,
play their interminable games of bridge which Edward must
never be allowed to lose. Throughout the remainder of the
year, they would never be apart for long. They weekended
together constantly—often with noble Mr. Keppel in the
party; and the King rapidly became part of the Keppel family
as well, frequently dining at their house in Portman Square
and acting as a sort of uncle to the Keppels' two young
daughters. They called him "Kingy," and were permitted to
race slices of buttered toast down his trouser legs when he
was sitting in their nursery.

Clearly in Mrs. Keppel, Edward the Rake had met his
match—the one woman in his life who could manage him
just as she seems to have managed almost everyone she met.
Largely thanks to her the last years of his regal, rakish life
were not quite the unhappy anticlimax that they might have
been.

Thanks to his immortal mother, he had been kept from
power too long to know how to use it when it came to him.
Thanks also to his worthy parents, he had been made the
lifelong rake he was, a social despot but a political nonentity.
He was a kindly king, and very popular, but he could hardly
be expected to have changed his life sufficiently to cope with
the new forces and new politicians of the explosive new
century in which he reigned. The Asquiths and Lloyd Georges
and young Winston Churchills were beyond him, and he
could never hope to have the sort of hold upon his century
that Victoria had had on hers. He must have known this. He
was emphatically no fool, and possibly this knowledge was

the cause of the depressions and despair that gradually assailed him.

But as with all rakes who survive to old age, he had at least the consolation of his misspent years. He had his memories and more than that, he still had his mistresses, a functioning digestion, and virility, three royal residences, a more or less devoted Empire, and half a million pounds a year. What other rake could say as much?

And in the long term, Edward's rakishness is not without historical importance. For he, and he alone, is the real bridge between the still powerful personal monarchy of the nineteenth century and the ceremonial and constitutional kingship of today. Had he been tougher, more politically skilled, less frivolous, and less of a rake, he might have found the time to fight battles for the monarchy which he could never hope to win. Luckily he had no chance, and the self-indulgent life he lived was the best turn he could possibly have done his subjects and the British monarchy.

When he died on Friday, May 6, 1910, Mrs. Keppel, who the day before had taken leave of her royal lover at the Palace, was herself prostrate with grief. The curtains in the house in Portman Square were pulled, and one of her young daughters asked her father why everyone was so upset because the King had died.

"Because," the Honorable George replied in what must surely be the most generous epitaph a man could give his wife's dead lover, "Kingy was a very, very wonderful person."

And so, in a way, he was.

Author's Note

Such a heavy curtain of official discretion was drawn across the private life of Edward during his life and at his death—at the accession of George V the chimneys of Buckingham Palace smoked for days as compromising papers of the dead king were systematically destroyed—that the full story of his half-century of pleasure never will be told. The details that exist have to be pieced together from a variety of books upon the period.

Among those which I have found particularly useful I must mention:

Benson, E. F. *As We Were.* Longmans, 1930.

Benson, E. F. *King Edward VII.* Longmans (Toronto), 1934.

Cowles, Virginia. *Gay Monarch: The Life and Pleasures of Edward VII.* Harper, 1956.

Lang, Theo. *The Darling Daisy Affair.* Atheneum, 1966.

Langtry, Lillie. *The Days I Knew*. Doran, 1925.

Lee, Sir Sidney. *King Edward VII: A Biography*. Macmillan, 1925–27.

Leslie, Anita. *The Marlborough House Set*. Doubleday, 1973.

Longford, Elizabeth. *Victoria R.I.* Weidenfield, 1964.

Magnus-Allcroft, Sir Philip Montefiore. *King Edward the Seventh*. Dutton, 1964.

Maurois, André. *King Edward and His Times*. Appleton-Century, 1933.

Nowell-Smith, Simon, ed. *Edwardian England 1901–1914*. Oxford, 1964.

Pearsall, Ronald. *Edwardian Life and Leisure*. David & Charles.

Pless, Mary Theresa Olivia (Cornwallis-West). *Daisy, Princess of Pless*. Dutton, 1936.

Richardson, Joanna. *The Courtesans*. World, 1967.

Sewell, J. P. C., ed. *Personal Letters of King Edward VII*. Hutchinson, 1931.

Sykes, Christopher. *Four Studies in Loyalty*. Sloane, 1948.

Sysonby, Frederick Edward Grey Ponsonby. *Recollections of Three Reigns*. Dutton, 1952.

Watson, A. E. D. *King Edward VII as a Sportsman*. Longmans, 1911.

Index